THE EQUITY/EXCELLENCE IMPERATIVE

A 2030 BLUEPRINT FOR UNDERGRADUATE EDUCATION AT U.S. RESEARCH UNIVERSITIES

THE EQUITY/EXCELLENCE IMPERATIVE

A 2030 BLUEPRINT FOR UNDERGRADUATE EDUCATION AT U.S. RESEARCH UNIVERSITIES

The Boyer 2030 Commission

The Association for Undergraduate Education
at Research Universities

The Association for Undergraduate Education at Research Universities (UERU), Fort Collins, CO 80523

ISBN 978-1-64215-150-3 (PDF) | 978-1-64215-151-0 (ePub) | 978-1-64642-386-6 (hardcover)

DOI 10.37514/CUS-B.2022.1503

Produced in the United States of America by The WAC Clearinghouse (wac.colostate.edu) and University Press of Colorado (upcolorado.com).

Library of Congress Cataloging-in-Publication Data available upon request.

Copyeditor: Karen Peirce
Designer: Mike Palmquist
Cover Art: John Gravdahl

About the Publisher: The Association for Undergraduate Education at Research Universities (ueru.org) is a Boyer-inspired university consortium, founded in 2000, hosted by Colorado State University since 2013, and dedicated to innovation on behalf of equity/excellence in undergraduate education at U.S. research universities.

Artist's Statement: "My goal for the design of the new 2030 Boyer Commission Blueprint was to echo gently the spirit of the same task given to Milton Glaser on the cover of the original 1998 Boyer Report. I focused on the use of the spiral plant, continuing its metaphorical reference to growth, movement, and vitality. In world history, spirals are often used to represent many philosophical expressions of life's journey. More recently, we see them in microscopic and cosmic natural science references. My abstraction of a growing vine strives to embrace that diversity. The inside and outside of the new column also give me a chance to suggest scholarship and community winding together where the colors change with each turn. It is an ascending journey."

Open-Access: This book is available in open-access digital format at ueru.org/boyer2030.

Land Acknowledgment. The Colorado State University Land Acknowledgment can be found at https://landacknowledgment.colostate.edu.

Support: The Commission expresses its gratitude for the generous support of the Raikes Foundation and the Suder Foundation.

Contents

Foreword

Dear Colleague,

Why a Boyer 2030 Commission? The world has changed since the Carnegie Foundation commissioned the landmark 1998 Boyer Commission Report, *Reinventing Undergraduate Education: A Blueprint for America's Research Universities* (https://tinyurl.com/3wc499s8), a manifesto calling for the "reinvention" of undergraduate education at U.S. research universities. A litany is suggestive: from climate change to climate emergency; from concern with inequalities to Black Lives Matter and renewed focus on equity; from deepening social divisions and distrust to worldwide threats to democracy itself. Add to this the COVID-19 pandemic and it is clear we face a panoply of critical challenges, democratic solutions to which require educated and engaged citizenries.

Founded originally to support implementation of the 1998 Boyer Report, The Association for Undergraduate Education at Research Universities (UERU) convened the Boyer 2030 Commission in 2021 to examine undergraduate education at U.S. research universities in light of the changes in the nearly 25 intervening years since the original report and in hope of seizing anticipated post-pandemic opportunities for progress in this critical area of higher education.

The time is now to renew and revitalize commitment to undergraduate education. In this report, the Boyer 2030 Commission outlines a compelling agenda for U.S. research universities to fundamentally enhance the distinctive educations that they provide for undergraduate students.

Co-chaired by Barbara R. Snyder and Peter McPherson (retired August 2022), the presidents of the Association of American Universities (AAU) and the Association of Public and Land-grant Universities (APLU), respectively, the Boyer 2030 Commission comprises 16 members whose considerable experience, expertise, and institutional positions speak directly to essential issues.

UERU hopes that this report, *The Equity/Excellence Imperative: A 2030 Blueprint for Undergraduate Education at U.S. Research Universities,* will aid leaders as they work to meet the imperative here described, and that millions of undergraduate students, not to mention their alma maters and broader human society, will meaningfully and measurably benefit as a result. UERU doesn't only hope: our members—public and private research universities that serve over 2.5 million undergraduate students annually (see Appendix C)—are dedicated to *the work* of the equity/excellence imperative. We invite others to join in these broadly collaborative efforts.

Sincerely,

Steven P. Dandaneau, Ph.D.
UERU Executive Director

⚡ The Boyer 2030 Commission

The Boyer 2030 Commission is a diverse group of accomplished higher education leaders whose experience and expertise grant them particular insight and purchase on undergraduate education at U.S. research universities. They are university presidents/chancellors, leaders of major higher education organizations, and eminent scholars and teachers across the range of disciplines from law to education, from the sciences to the arts, from the humanities to the social sciences. Their collective experience spans public and private higher education, government, and industry. Chaired by Barbara R. Snyder, president of AAU, and Peter McPherson, president of APLU, the Commission was convened by the Association for Undergraduate Education at Research Universities (UERU) to revisit and update the landmark 1998 Boyer Report. In this new report, the Boyer 2030 Commission advocates urgent reform organized around "the equity/excellence imperative."

Co-Chairs

Barbara R. Snyder, President, AAU   **Peter McPherson**, President Emeritus, APLU

Commission Members

Michael Crow, President, Arizona State University

Andrew Delbanco, President, Teagle Foundation

Roger Ferguson, former President, TIAA-CREF

Kathleen Fitzpatrick, Director of Digital Humanities, Michigan State University

Kevin Kruger, President and CEO, NASPA–Student Affairs Administrators in Higher Education

Gary May, Chancellor, University of California, Davis

Sarah Newman, Director of Art and Education at metaLAB, Harvard University

Lynn Pasquerella, President, American Association of Colleges & Universities (AAC&U)

Deborah Santiago, Co-Founder and CEO, *Excelencia* in Education

Claude Steele, Lucie Stern Professor in the Social Sciences, Emeritus, Stanford University

Holden Thorp, Editor-in-Chief, *Science*

Eric Waldo, Founding Executive Director of Michelle Obama's Reach Higher

Mary Wright, Associate Provost for Teaching and Learning, Brown University

Ex officio: **Elizabeth Loizeaux**, Boston University; Former President, UERU

Staff

Liz Bennett, Associate Director, UERU

Steven Dandaneau, Executive Director, UERU

Howard Gobstein, Senior Vice President, APLU

Ken Goldstein, Senior Vice President, AAU

Tara King, Education Program and Evaluation Manager, AAU

Emily Miller, Deputy Vice President, AAU

Mariah Pursley, Senior Coordinator, UERU

Kacy Redd, Associate Vice President, APLU

Liz Wasden, Research Assistant, University of Maryland, College Park

THE EQUITY/EXCELLENCE IMPERATIVE

A 2030 BLUEPRINT FOR UNDERGRADUATE
EDUCATION AT U.S. RESEARCH UNIVERSITIES

Executive Summary

Research university presidents/chancellors, provosts, and their senior colleagues are today called upon to lead in a challenging world of deeply entrenched inequities laid bare by a deadly pandemic; a long-overdue racial reckoning; fractured democratic institutions and frayed democratic norms; an existential planetary climate emergency; a mental health crisis affecting all ages, including and especially traditional-aged undergraduate students; and growing public disaffection with and distrust of higher education. College-going and the prestige of a college degree are in decline, and, despite efforts to recruit and retain low-income undergraduate students, new data show that research universities were serving even fewer of them prior to the pandemic, let alone as a result.[1]

The Boyer 2030 Commission Report is organized around what the Commission has termed the "equity/excellence imperative," a belief that excellence and equity are inextricably entwined, such that excellence without equity (privilege reproducing privilege) is not true excellence, and equity (mere access) without excellence is unfulfilled promise.

At this pivotal moment, the Boyer 2030 Commission poses this fundamental question:

How can U.S. research universities embrace the equity/excellence imperative?

- Can we commit to *equity* as a necessary and defining precondition of *excellence*?
- Can we conceive, prioritize, and invest in equitable undergraduate achievement?
- Can we educate and support undergraduates for 21st-century world readiness?

Meeting the equity/excellence imperative offers a leadership opportunity. Recognizing that diversity of mission, identity, organization, and culture is a long-standing strength of U.S. higher education, the Boyer 2030 Commission offers 11 provocations to catalyze the multiple actions needed for a research university to realize the equity/excellence imperative:

I. **World Readiness for All: Education for Life, Work, and Citizenship**
   1. **World Readiness:** Will we prioritize transformative education for life, work, and citizenship in an age of daunting challenges in need of world-embracing solutions? Will we ensure such education for *all* students, not only those already privileged?
   2. **Freedom of Speech and Expression in Supportive Campus Cultures:** How can we nurture trust within university communities and build student capacity for leadership in democratic society?

II. **Equity/Excellence in Teaching and Learning**
   3. **Access to Excellence:** How can we render high-impact practices—hallmarks of excellence—accessible to all?
   4. **Teaching:** How will we ensure that our students—all of them, without exception—are educated using evidence-informed pedagogies in intentionally inclusive and empathy-based environments?
   5. **Advising:** How can we ensure that all students receive excellent advising—*holistic* advising that is student-centered and encompasses academic, career, and basic needs guidance—so students can best benefit from our complex institutions?
   6. **Faculty Rewards and Structure:** How can we best recognize, support, and reward faculty across all appointment types for the expertise and dedication they bring to achieving equitable, excellent undergraduate education?

III. Facilitating Success/Eliminating Barriers

7. **Access and Affordability:** How can we recruit and best support undergraduates from diverse communities and include them in research universities' empowering academic programs and myriad scholarly projects aimed at advancing the quality of human experience in the US and worldwide?

8. **Degree Pathways:** How can we identify curricular and other opportunities to facilitate degree completion at our universities—and leverage and enhance them? How can we identify curricular and other similarly institutionalized barriers to degree completion—and remove them?

9. **Digital Technology:** How can we use technology strategically and in financially sustainable ways to ambitiously scale up equity/excellence in undergraduate education?

IV. Fostering Belonging and Equitable Campus Cultures

10. **Nurturing Mental Health and Well-Being:** How can we urgently support belonging and wellness in the university community? How can we identify and eliminate policies or practices that exacerbate mental health problems, which disproportionately affect students from underrepresented groups (including first-generation, low-income, and students of color)?

V. Leading Change

11. **Assessment and Accountability:** How can we best assess our progress toward meeting the equity/excellence imperative? How should we hold ourselves accountable?

Introduction

The Boyer 2030 Commission believes that *now* is the time for research universities to invest in and strengthen undergraduate education. We must make undergraduate students the priority we claim they are and know they must be. While marshaling the motivation and allocating the funding required amidst other important claims on resources will no doubt be challenging, such mobilization and investment will be amply repaid by a more robust and effective democratic citizenry and a diverse 21st-century workforce better equipped to meet the multifaceted challenges of our time. Prioritizing undergraduate education is also the best means for research universities to increase annual net revenue and help renew much-needed public trust. Prioritizing undergraduate education works on many levels and fosters many virtuous circles, but the bottom line is that the equity/excellence imperative in undergraduate education drives university growth and development and is key to overall success. In short, we can do well while we do good.

There are reasons to be optimistic. Our response to the COVID-19 pandemic demonstrated that we *can* change; the resulting experiments undertaken in digital learning, admissions, and academic policies, to name only a few areas of recent innovation, provide valuable insights about possible new ways forward. As a sector, research universities are poised to redouble fundamental reform efforts and to eschew incremental gains in favor of qualitative institutional and cultural change. Because research universities are higher education leaders, they are poised to lead widespread innovation.

The kind of action needed is clear and underway. The 1998 Boyer Commission Report already pressed the need for fundamental change in how research universities educate undergraduates. In direct and indirect response to that report, U.S. research universities conceived and launched exemplary undergraduate research and living-learning programs, established centers for teaching and learning to advance new and promising pedagogical innovations, and developed first-year programs that include small classes, to name a few improvements.[2] Student orientation leaders no longer direct new matriculants to "look to your left, look to your right" to see who will not make it to graduation, while students avail themselves of a wealth of "high-impact practices" in addition to, and within, standard course work.[3] Undergraduate education *has* improved and research universities have come to appreciate their vested interest in attracting undergraduate students to distinctive, transformative educations.

> ## What is distinctive about an undergraduate education at a research university?
>
> - Undergraduate students are immersed in a culture of inquiry, discovery, and creativity via introduction to state-of-the-art knowledge and to the most compelling questions and most exciting frontiers of learning.
> - Undergraduates are immersed in the creation of new ideas, new scientific discoveries, and new artistic works—from which they learn and to which they can themselves contribute within a community of world-class educators, researchers and scholars, fellow undergraduates, graduate students, and post-doctoral fellows.
> - Undergraduates benefit from a vast array of academic fields to explore and choose among for in-depth study and from the unparalleled diversity of fellow students with and from whom they learn and grow.

Yet not all students have equitable access to the advancements of the past 20 years, nor are those advances consistently construed and supported. This reality, combined with a rapidly changing world, requires not that we begin afresh, but that we double down on the original Boyer Commission's call for fundamental reform.

The Boyer 2030 Commission believes that U.S. research universities can and must deliver empowering, life-enhancing higher education for the millions of undergraduate students who seek it and for those who would matriculate and succeed were our institutions fully accessible, inclusive, and just.

Enrollment Trends

Undergraduate student enrollment at 4-year public and private research universities is increasingly racially and ethnically diverse, yet a majority of undergraduates continue to identify racially as White. The most pronounced enrollment shifts are increases in the number of Hispanic students (variously self-identified) at public research universities (R1 and R2) and international students at private very high research universities (R1). See Figure 1.

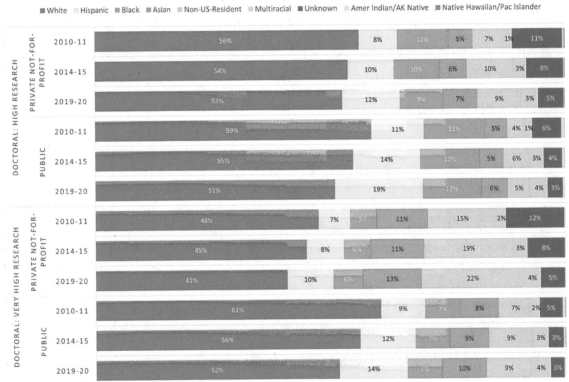

Figure 1. Percentage distribution of 12-month enrollment at 4-year public and not-for-profit institutions by student race/ethnicity, institutional context, and year.

Six-Year Completion Rates

Six-year completion rates at research universities ranged from 61% (R2) to 77% (R1) in 2019. These completion rates have increased over time, and research universities as a group continue to outperform all 4-year degree-granting institutions as a group. When disaggregating the data by demographics, however, 6-year completion rates for Black and Hispanic students are significantly lower than they are for White students at research universities (R1 and R2) and across all 4-year institutions. See Figure 2.

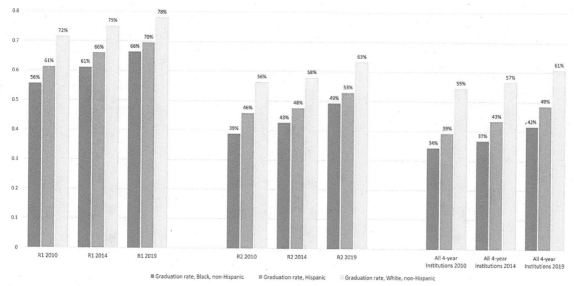

Figure 2. Graduation rates over time of selected demographics by Carnegie Classification.

Pell Grant Recipients

The enrollment of Pell grant recipients at research universities (R1 and R2) as well as across all 4-year institutions has slightly decreased over the years, which is a concern. In 2019, 28% of students received Pell grants at public and private research universities (R1 and R2), whereas at all 4-year institutions, 33% of students received Pell grants. In 2019, the 6-year completion rate for Pell grant recipients at very high research universities (R1) was 71% compared to 54% at high research universities (R2). Across all 4-year institutions, the 6-year completion rate for Pell grant recipients was lower than for non-Pell recipients. See Figures 3 and 4.

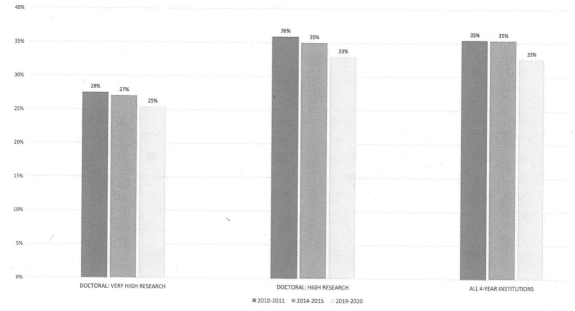

Figure 3. Pell awardees as a percentage of total undergraduates by Carnegie Classification: Fall 2010, Fall 2014, and Fall 2018.

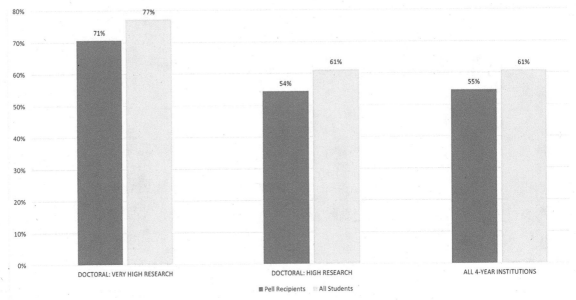

Figure 4. Six-year graduation rates by Pell status and Carnegie Classification 2019.

Guiding Principle: Equity and Excellence are Inextricably Entwined

This report is organized around what the Boyer 2030 Commission has termed the "equity/excellence imperative," which is grounded in a belief that excellence and equity are inextricably entwined, such that excellence without equity (privilege reproducing privilege) is not true excellence, and equity (mere access) without excellence is unfulfilled promise. Research universities have an opportunity in this pandemic-disrupted period to help lead higher education and, indeed, U.S. society, toward increased equity/excellence and strengthened democracy.

— ◆ —

Let's redefine excellence in a way that doesn't involve ranking and sorting of students but views excellence as a process and one that's centered on equity.

— Lynn Pasquerella, AAC&U President,
Boyer 2030 Commissioner

It is not true that universities can have equity only at the expense of excellence—and excellence only at the expense of equity. What if excellence were defined as the difference between what a student entered and left college with? Areas of growth might include breadth and depth of knowledge, the ability to marshal evidence to make complex arguments and express them well, the ability to apply knowledge to new situations, the skills to work well with diverse others, the freedom of mind and creativity to think differently and imaginatively. What if one measure of excellence were a graduation rate that beat the odds as set by the status quo—and what if all students regardless of family and community background graduated having been supported, challenged, and transformed by what they'd learned? What if we coupled such measures with assessment of life purpose and career satisfaction decades on?

We must not accept the false, invidious trade-off between equity and excellence. Democracy entails the opposite.

— ❧ —

Our students and our institutions are harmed by the notion that selectivity on admission is quality from a priori point of initiation, which it isn't . . . that somehow if you're going to Cal State Fullerton and studying engineering because you somehow didn't get into UCLA you're a lesser person and a lesser faculty member when you're not.

– Michael Crow, President of Arizona State University,
Boyer 2030 Commissioner

The Boyer 2030 Commission recognizes that defining excellence in terms of equity rather than, for example, selectivity and sorting, unsettles at least 70 years of practice. Excellence founded in equity requires us to think differently about *why* we do what we do, not only what we do and how we do it. Change of this magnitude, and subtlety, will not be easy nor without significant complication, but some leaders are already finding ways to center equity in their pursuit of excellence, while many—surely most others—are attuned to what is needed and eager to engage. Such leaders are laudable and inspiring, and we highlight and celebrate some of their work here. The Boyer 2030 Commission believes that the US can continue to lead the world in higher education and fulfill its public mission *only* by realizing equity as a precondition of excellence.

A Note on Language

Language matters. This report's use of inclusive language is guided by University Press of Colorado standards and informed by the Boyer 2030 Commission's understanding that language is a contested and always-changing medium. On the one hand, like all social structures, language reflects established mindsets and power relations, and, on the other, it can facilitate social and cultural change. Few today would think to use "man" to mean "humanity." Recently, Howard Hughes Medical Institute's David Asai offered the term "PEERs"—persons excluded because of their ethnicity or race—to draw attention as well as simultaneously propose a solution to a key dimension of institutional discrimination as it is experienced in everyday practice. The Boyer 2030 Commission understands that the language choices made in this report, whether by experts we quote or in the words of the Commission, are made with intention to recognize and promote change and are likely to be superseded by future advances.[92]

Eleven Provocations for Equity/ Excellence

The Boyer 2030 Commission urges the senior leadership of research universities to place undergraduate students at the center of thinking about reform efforts: Who are our undergraduate students and how can we meet them where they are? What, in other words, do they need to thrive, graduate, and make successful transitions to life after college? What do they need in order to live meaningful lives, pursue work they value, and participate effectively in democratic self-governance? How can research universities—with their rich complement of faculty and staff engaged in research, teaching, and co- and extracurricular activities—best ensure an excellent education for all?

The following enumerated provocations are meant to stimulate institutional and cultural change.

— ✦ —

Excellence is not pristine. It's messy. Allow that vulnerability.

– Sarah Newman, Director of Art and Education at
metaLAB (https://mlml.io) at Harvard University,
Boyer 2030 Commissioner

I. World Readiness for All: Education for Life, Work, and Citizenship

1. World Readiness: Will we prioritize transformative education for life, work, and citizenship in an age of daunting challenges in need of world-embracing solutions? Will we ensure such education for *all* students, not only those already privileged?

The equity/excellence imperative demands that we educate for "world readiness." This is the term the Boyer 2030 Commission borrows from Cathy Davidson, founding director of The Futures Initiative at the City University of New York, to articulate a vision of undergraduate education that includes and goes beyond the essential goal of near-term workforce readiness to empower students for citizenship, life, *and* work throughout their lifetimes.[4] This is not an either-or proposition: universities must do both—transformative education and preparation for that first, post-college step—and they must do them both well. Education for world readiness must be coherent, transparent, and explicit in purpose. It must simultaneously prepare undergraduates for life as productive citizens *and* economic actors where the best way to do both is to prepare students for life itself—life in our times and with an anticipated future in mind, which is to say, for *world readiness*.

Education for "world readiness" is 21st-century education that broadens horizons, stimulates curiosity and involves discovery of fields of knowledge, ways of knowing, and perspectives well beyond what most students have encountered in high school. It provides students the experience of grappling with complex problems and seeking nuanced understandings. It develops students' knowledge of, and respect for, those whose views may differ from theirs and for epistemologies and methodologies—knowledge claims writ large—that initially may seem opaque. It teaches students how to learn and fosters humility in the face of what they do not yet know. A 21st-century descendant of what has traditionally been called "liberal education," such broad education is essential for many reasons, including readying students to flourish as self-directed learners.

"Liberal and practical education" both: this is what the Morrill Act of 1862 establishing many of our current land-grant universities explicitly deemed essential—the world readiness of its day.[5]

To be clear about terms and avoid common misunderstanding: the Boyer 2030 Commission agrees with the AAC&U (https://www.aacu.org) that "the antithesis of liberal education is not conservative education but illiberal education—indoctrination, rote and purely instrumental learning, unquestioned transmission of a closed system of thought."[6]

— ✦ —

What's increasingly rare in higher education, and almost entirely missing from writings about its future, is a more than nominal commitment to the value of learning undertaken in the hope of expanding the sympathetic imagination by opening the mind to contesting ideas about nature and history, the power of literature and art, and the value of dialectic in the pursuit of truth. These aspirations—traditionally gathered under the term "liberal education"—are in desperate need of revival. To advance them requires teachers and institutions committed to a more capacious vision of education than the prevailing idea of workforce training and economic self-advancement.

– Andrew Delbanco, President, Teagle Foundation, Boyer 2030 Commissioner[7]

Equity

The current public and policy discourse tends to isolate and privilege short-term economic benefit and increasingly promotes illiberal forms of postsecondary education—recasting higher education as a private rather than a public good; undermining its broader civic, democratic, and cultural aims; reducing sharply the expectations of students and other stakeholders; and, ultimately, threatening to reproduce socioeconomic stratification.

—AAC&U[8]

The equity/excellence imperative requires wide-ranging educational experiences for all students. The implications of this notion are profound for students and for faculty and the universities that support them both. The Boyer 2030 Commission emphasizes, as does Roosevelt Montás, former director of the core curriculum at Columbia University, that the prevailing narrative that renders a rich and transforming general education a dispensable luxury is both "pervasive *and paternalistic* [emphasis added]."[9] This false narrative signals to many students, especially those who are low-income, immigrant, and first-generation (all three true of Dr. Montás when he was an undergraduate), that a broad education generally and the arts and humanities particularly are not for them. Such discriminatory paternalism is unacceptable.

Michael Lomax, president and CEO of the United Negro College Fund, strikes a similar note about equity/excellence in higher education: "It's more than the urgency of getting something beyond a living wage. It's the urgency of economic independence, but it's also the urgency I find in our students and their families to develop themselves fully."[10] Davidson adds further observation of widespread desire for broader social impact and personal growth, documenting that her "students who come from the most precarious personal backgrounds . . . want something more [than a job]: a career, a vocation, a life path, a way to contribute, a way to make themselves and their families proud and their communities strong. They don't just want a skill for a changing world. They want to be changemakers.[11]

Democracy and social justice demand world readiness for all. While most need gainful employment, that is not all they need.

Recent research suggests that, even before the pandemic, student disengagement was widespread (about 30% of students reported being disengaged), and that more and more students think of college as merely a transaction by which one obtains a credential. This attitude discourages intellectual exploration and leads students simply to go through the motions: acquire a diploma, get a job.[12] Transactional attitudes and anxiety-induced, short-horizon focus on career outcomes, and on first jobs particularly, do not envision the needed education for leadership, lifelong learning, and engaged citizenry. *This* status quo is out of step with both societal and individual needs.[13] World readiness is language meant to inspire change.

The Humanities

U.S. higher education is threatened by efforts to defund transformative education and otherwise limit what can be said—indeed, what can be *studied*. The misleading narrative that "you can't get a job with an art history major" and other such invalid claims about the relative value of academic and professional disciplines discourages students from studying the arts and humanities, as well as some of the natural sciences, and drives them toward fields perceived as a more direct path to a job. This helps precipitate as well as perpetuate shrinking enrollments in fields most invested in cultivating transformative education, and in humanities departments particularly. The deleterious effect of such trends, whether direct and intentional or indirect and collateral, has risen to a crisis both alarming and consequential.

Indeed, the precipitous decline in the humanities comes at the very moment when the central substance of those fields—cross-cultural understanding; ethics; the pursuit of meaning; communication of complex, nuanced ideas; critical thinking—are desperately needed both for providing the purchase on enduring human questions so necessary for mental health and a fulfilling life and for effectively addressing society's most pressing problems. Turning the tide on global climate change, racism, poverty, and authoritarian threats to democracy depends on changing societies *and* cultures—what humans value, how they behave, and why.[14]

All the scientific and technological skills of which we can conceive will not solve our world problems if we do not build and adapt a base of human and cultural understanding; ethical and moral underpinnings; sensible rules of law for the 21st century; and integration with the insights, inspirations, and communications of the arts.

– Charles M. Vest, President, National Academy of Engineering.[15]

Career Preparation

The ideal of being a lifelong learner is no longer a platitude. It has become an economic necessity, and the academic community is only beginning to understand that traditional teaching methods and curricula must be adapted to develop a twenty-first-century workforce and citizens of an increasingly complex world.

—Buck Goldstein and Holden Thorp, Editor, *Science*,
Boyer 2030 Commissioner[16]

Most undergraduate students bank on their university educations to prepare and position them for rewarding careers.[17] Career preparation is key to their motivation to matriculate and their determination to fulfill degree program requirements, and it is nothing about which anyone should be surprised, much less chagrined. Education for world readiness prepares students for long-term career success—education for students' last jobs, as Rachel Croson, Provost, University of Minnesota, explains to her university's constituents. Communication about the purpose of education for world readiness must convey the fact that educators and employers are closely aligned on how higher education should prepare students. Employers value the skills, knowledge, and habits of mind developed by an excellent general education, e.g., oral and written communication, critical thinking, ethical judgment, working effectively in diverse groups, and application of skills and knowledge.[18]

Business leaders today are looking for a diversity of skills, and not just technical knowledge. Pivotal right now in financial services—a relationship business—is trust built around empathy, understanding, listening skills, critical thinking. It's not enough in financial services to simply be able to work with a spreadsheet. You need to convince your individual or institutional clients to take the right set of actions. The skills that come out of the humanities, the softer relationship skills—listening, empathy, an appreciation for context—are incredibly important. Of the individuals in my organization who receive the most consistently positive feedback—who are most valued by our clients . . . Most of them learned their financial activities at our firm, but came into the firm with a much broader range of skills.

– Roger Ferguson, former President and CEO,
TIAA-CREF, Boyer 2030 Commissioner[19]

CAREER EXPLORATION AND PREPARATION

In February 2022, The **University of California, Davis** (UC Davis) announced a major new initiative to make career exploration and preparation accessible to all students as a matter of equity and social justice: Aggie Launch (https://tinyurl.com/4d7u6e57). Aggie Launch focuses on both preparation for career *and* connection to first job. For example, the Aggie Square innovation hub (https://aggiesquare.ucdavis.edu) will bring together "leading-edge UC Davis research, innovative companies and startups, and talent from across [the] community." Aiming "to remove barriers to student participation—including awareness about opportunities, finances, and lack of transportation to jobs and internships," Aggie Launch involves the whole campus.

Education for world readiness supports new college graduates as they enter full-time employment and begin professional careers. World readiness includes workforce readiness. Preprofessional and professional education as well as career counseling are essential aspects of transformative education and academic guidance, where transition to a career path is of equal significance to initial transition to the university and choice of academic majors and minors. All three are decisive turning points in a typical undergraduate career and need intentional integration. That integration must include high-impact practices (HIPs) such as undergraduate research, professional internships, and community-engaged learning, which are now essential for most students' short- and long-term career prospects. Expanding education abroad and internationalizing the domestic curricula are, not surprisingly, also necessary for world readiness and are consistent with employers' needs and expectations in an era of globalization and its concomitant increase in boundaryless competition for employee/employer excellence.

When developing initiatives to make career exploration and preparation accessible to all students, such as "Aggie Launch" at UC Davis, we knew it was important to involve the whole campus. Beyond the career center, there needs to be a campus-wide fleet of partners across both academic and administrative units in students' career preparation, an infrastructure that supports them in existing programs as well as in opportunities such as integrated classroom learning and community engagement, and work-study in partnership with innovative new startups and small businesses. We want undergraduate and graduate students to know they have resources on campus and people who want to help them be successful in starting their career preparations early, participating in an expanded array of experiential learning, benefiting from career mentoring, and graduating with a robust career plan or path to advanced studies.

– Gary S. May, Chancellor of the University of California, Davis, Boyer 2030 Commissioner

General Education

Education for world readiness is accomplished through degree programs as a whole, typically made up of three or four essential parts: university-wide general education or core curriculum requirements, major or concentration requirements, sometimes college or school-level requirements, and electives. Co- and extracurricular activities also play important roles for world readiness and should be aligned intentionally with its goals.

Despite the diversity of research universities, every research university supports faculty who integrate teaching, research, and service and who provide undergraduate students with much more than the opportunity to specialize in academic and professional disciplines. The typical U.S. research university devotes roughly one third of the credits in its undergraduate degree programs to core curricula or general education (by various names). This is the primary means of cultivating world readiness, though not, as noted, its exclusive preserve.

Few provosts, however, are confident that students understand the purpose of general education.[20] And not all university general education programs are required of all students. Many students—in pursuit of efficiency and savings and sometimes simply in response to disrupted lives and few resources available to mitigate life's challenges—pursue general education via ad hoc, piecemeal, and otherwise fragmentary pathways, just to "get it out of the way." Some professional degree programs formally exempt courses in the humanities, social sciences, and arts that would better prepare students for professional careers in a world where viable solutions often require multiple disciplinary and cultural perspectives, along with vision, imagination, creativity, communication skills, and critical self-awareness.

The fact that general education courses are embedded in curricula across departments is germane to education for world readiness. This embeddedness is a strength in that it conserves accumulated knowledge, tradition, and perhaps even enduring wisdom. But embeddedness can also challenge adaptation to significantly altered circumstances and new educational needs. The last includes the equity/excellence imperative.

The quantity of information now accessible online is unprecedented; social media is impacting the way people think and communicate. How can we prepare students to be critical consumers of online information, to feel empowered, and to know their rights? Our institutions can do better to educate our students in this capacity.

— Sarah Newman, Director of Art and Education at metaLAB, Harvard, Boyer 2030 Commissioner

REDESIGNING GENERAL EDUCATION

Implemented in fall 2018, the BU Hub (https://tinyurl.com/4hfncmav) is **Boston University**'s (BU) first university-wide general education program for all students in its eleven undergraduate schools and colleges. It emphasizes the connections among disciplines as students develop six essential capacities-- the knowledge, skills, and habits of mind they need to thrive in a complex, diverse world. Students pursue the Hub across all four years, in the major and out, in the classroom and in cocurricular activities and other innovative learning experiences, such as the Cross-College Challenge, a team-taught, multi-disciplinary team project.

The Boyer 2030 Commission wholeheartedly agrees with one undergraduate vice provost who responded to the 2021 Association for Undergraduate Education at Research Universities (UERU) survey of its member institutions: "Most of us, including my own institution, are running with distribution models of general education that reach back to the mid-20th-century (requirement tweaks and various re-naming/re-labeling initiatives notwithstanding). It's time for a reconsideration." (See Appendix A for the full text of the survey and a sampling of results.)

Setting the goals, structure, and content of education for world readiness—and making explicit and transparent the possible pathways students can take in its pursuit (see #8: Degree Pathways, later in this report)—is one of the major responsibilities of the faculty in collaboration with their partners in student affairs.

The Boyer 2030 Commission celebrates world readiness as a vision that centers transformative education as essential to higher education and to societal needs. There is no such thing as a research university undergraduate student—regardless of background, academic specialization, or life and career ambitions—who may safely "get gen ed out of the way" or treat a university education as just another box to check. Our world is arguably one of uncertain prospects, with great opportunities vying with great challenges, where the knowledge and skills that best prepare one for a first job must be accompanied by those needed to then adjust and adapt. From a world readiness point of view, liberal education *is* career preparation.

Strategies

◢ The equity/excellence imperative requires that research universities collectively and individually develop action and communication plans to rewrite the increasingly entrenched public view of university education that pits general education *against* career readiness. Students and society need both. We need to prepare students for their first jobs and for world readiness. To repeat: it is not a question of either/or. We need to do both and do both well. Headwinds may be strong on campus as well as off. Achieving this goal will require persistence along with consistent, ongoing action and communication to all stakeholders about world readiness and the value of an education that cultivates the knowledge and habits of mind students need to live thoughtfully, participate effectively in self-governance, and pursue lifetimes of meaningful work, while also preparing them for those crucial first post-college career steps.

 Consider reviewing and revising your general education/core curriculum. Universities would do well to ask: Is our current core curriculum/general education program a powerful, potentially transformative educational experience that provides students orientation to the world that is their inheritance? The questions in Appendix B are offered as possible prompts for conversation.

 Integrate, integrate, integrate. Core curricula and general education by whatever name and type must be coherent, transparent, and explicit in purpose. The pathways through degree programs must be as clear as their goals, and those goals must be compellingly relevant to the world students will help shape. Students must be able to *see* interrelationships among courses, among the parts of their degree program, and between what they do in the classroom and out of the classroom.

 Undergraduates, especially traditional-aged students relatively lacking in professional work experience, benefit from early introduction to career opportunities that are then reinforced throughout their undergraduate experience via course work, high-impact learning, holistic advising, and co- and extracurricular activities.[21] Such preparation should culminate in engagement with career counseling professionals who assist students in transitioning successfully to initial employment or, for those interested in postbaccalaureate education, with faculty and other expert advisors. Alumni networks and other connections to professional work provide additional support.

2. Freedom of Speech and Expression and Supportive Campus Cultures: How can we nurture trust within university communities and build student capacity for leadership in democratic society?

This is generous thinking: listening to one another, recognizing that we have as much to learn as we do to teach, finding ways to use our collective knowledge for the public good. From the broadest rethinking of our political and institutional landscape, to developing new ways of working in public, to sharing our ways of reading, to focusing on the most intimate practice of listening—at each level, we must be connected to, fully part of, the world around us.

– Kathleen Fitzpatrick, Director of Digital Humanities and
Professor of English, Michigan State University,
Boyer 2030 Commissioner[22]

STRENGTHENING COMMUNITY

Between 2019 and 2022, the **Student Experience Project** (SEP)—funded by the Raikes Foundation and organized on six university campuses with support of several national organizations, including APLU and its Coalition of Urban-Serving Universities (USU)—used social-psychological research and evidence-based practices to help instructors create equitable learning environment in STEM courses and foster belonging, trust, and self-efficacy among their students.[94] SEP produced positive results in course persistence and grades, especially for undergraduates from structurally disadvantaged groups (racial-ethnic minority students, women, students with financial stress, transfer students, and first-generation college students).[95] Research findings that flow from scholars like Claude Steele, Sylvia Hurtado, Carol Dweck, Estela Mara Bensimon, and Mary Murphy (a SEP PI) can help us to proactively cultivate inclusive and just campus communities, beginning in the classroom. Such academic-and-equity-driven reforms strengthen community and nurture campus cultures that support campus freedom of speech and expression. The instructional practices used in SEP are openly available for use (http://tinyurl.com/3aa7dehw). As SEP participant John Smail of the University of North Carolina at Charlotte, succinctly noted, "They work."

Among the thorniest but most important challenges facing campus communities is finding workable balancing points between freedom of speech and expression on the one hand, and the values of equality and community (experienced as security, trust, and mutual respect within university communities) on the other. Modern democracies have been striking this difficult balance, mostly with success, since their creations, managing over time attendant and probably unavoidable tensions and related swings of opinion.

The way forward may not be as clear as we would like.[23] But surely it involves affirming our commitment to freedom of speech and expression as well as building trust and understanding among members of university communities, especially in support of those most threatened and most vulnerable.

In preparation for this report, the Boyer 2030 Commission invited a presentation on free speech by Tony Frank, chancellor of the Colorado State University System and former president of the Colorado State University main campus in Fort Collins. At the end of his thoughtful remarks, grounded in the give-and-take of real-world campus experience, Boyer 2030 Commissioner and former provost at the University of California, Berkeley and dean of education at Stanford University, Claude Steele, asked Frank about our responsibilities to those who are the target of protected speech but whose membership in the university community—indeed, whose very existence as human beings—is sometimes implicitly if not explicitly threatened by that speech. Dr. Steele's perspective is worth quoting at length:

I believe that universities must affirm and protect freedom of speech and expression. The concern I have is this: For groups and identities that have traditionally been disenfranchised in the larger society but are now—over the last 50 or so years—being increasingly integrated into our institutions as we diversify them, there is an issue of trust: can people from these backgrounds and identities drop their guard and trust in the value of free speech when, sometimes, it has been used to license the expression of deeply devaluing ideas about them and their identities? In my own experience, I think of the years of open debate about whether African Americans were genetically inferior intellectually. The centrality of free speech to the integrity of university life is unassailable. But as our institutions diversify, those from previously excluded groups who still have experiences of devaluation in these institutions may wonder if they can trust it . . . . Can they trust and take this principle at face value, or should they worry that it could wind up licensing their devaluation in the setting—as it has in the past, and sometimes, continues to do so in the present. Our institutions will have to build more trusting relationships with students from these backgrounds before we can expect them to accept a broad principle like this without some worry and doubt. Importantly, it isn't the principle of free speech per se that is problematic for these students. It's the question of whether they can trust their safety in the institution enough to let down their guard and accept the principle involved at face value.

So, as we fully understand and accept how essential this principle is to our institutions, this is the reality of our moment. It is a moment that requires more than simply reasserting the essentialness of free speech to higher education. It requires both a recognition of the real dilemma the traditionally disenfranchised face in our institutions—that our history as a society is still quite with us—and some compelling approach to building their trust. As these students experience that kind of institutional understanding and responsiveness, their trust in a general principle like free speech may be more forthcoming.

I am optimistic on this point, because I believe that building that trust is not beyond our reach. When people recognize that an institution understands who they are and the dilemmas they face—material and psychological—and then extends itself to help them cope with these challenges and succeed in the institutions—I think of Georgia State as a good example of how to do this—people can more easily trust an institutional stress on free speech.

Note that the values of responsibility, maturity, and respect for judgment rooted in accumulated experience and critical self-reflection, sometimes called "conservative values," are truly values for everyone. Cultivated variously, we can hardly imagine undergraduate education at research universities surviving, much less thriving, without them. The Boyer 2030 Commission recommends renewed dedication to make our campuses places of diverse opinion that welcome freedom of speech and expression at the same time as we vigorously protect and indeed strengthen the security and standing of those historically excluded in higher education, and who are still often targets of violence and discrimination. The balancing may be unavoidable, but it is best undertaken *proactively* by cultivating sincerely and deeply held bonds of trust, understanding, and mutual respect for all communities. In this view, the equity/excellence imperative entails balancing freedom and responsibility, which is neither new nor threatening, at least not to those who are responsible nor for those who value basic freedoms.

Strategies

◆ Begin, suggests Ronald Daniels, president of Johns Hopkins University, by convening panels rather than individual speakers to model civil, open debate on controversial issues.[24]

◆ Andrew Delbanco, president of the Teagle Foundation and Boyer 2030 Commissioner, suggests the best forum is the classroom—not large crowds, not on social media—but in a classroom where students know each other's names: "Certain habits of mind—distinguishing between arguments and opinions, admitting self-doubt, rethinking assumptions—are," Delbanco argues, "imperative for collective life. If these habits are not nurtured in the college classroom, where else will they be found?"[25]

◆ Another promising avenue involves expanding the parameters of tolerance by reinstituting formal debates in which students argue positions they may not hold themselves and by starting with lower-stakes issues before proceeding to those more consequential.

◆ Promote freedom of speech and expression as a university *and* societal ideal.

II. Equity/Excellence in Teaching and Learning

Research universities are typically large, and occasionally extraordinarily large, institutions; they are organizationally complex and often decentralized and nuanced; they are composed of a multiplicity of subcultures intersecting with dominant cultures (including heterogeneous and, occasionally, peculiar academic cultures); U.S. research universities are overflowing with opportunities, pathways, and potentially overwhelming, as well as transformative, choices.

Undergraduate students hail from diverse and unequal backgrounds and pursue idiosyncratic futures; hidden curricula vie with those visible for students' attention, as do world events and popular culture. Students must select among overflowing opportunities, choose viable pathways, and make life-altering choices.

Designing intentional educational experiences and ensuring effective and equitable teaching for world readiness are critical for both quality of student learning and equitable degree completion.

3. Access to Excellence: How can we render high-impact practices—hallmarks of excellence—accessible to all?

Questions of access don't end when students are accepted to college. Are enriching educational experiences that are particularly beneficial accessible to all students? What is the *quality* of the education available to students?

We can approach those questions by considering the "high-impact practices" (HIPs)—hallmarks of transformative educational practices—that teach students the critical life and problem-solving skills they need to thrive outside the classroom. They include such experiences as first-year seminars, faculty-mentored research, study abroad, internships, and living-learning communities.[26] HIPs require considerable time and effort from students, meaningful interactions between students and faculty, collaboration among individuals with diverse perspectives, consistent feedback and iteration, real-world application and practice, and opportunities for reflection.[27] Some students especially benefit from these practices: for example, among students who participate in HIPs in their first year, studies show that "Black students' gains in first-to-second-year retention rates and Hispanic students' gains in first-year grade point averages (GPAs) are greater than those of white students."[28]

Though nearly 60% of students report engaging in at least two HIPs by the time they graduate, there are significant roadblocks to equitable access among marginalized student groups.[29] For example, the 2019 National Survey of Student Engagement (NSSE) found 51% of White students participated in an internship compared to 40% of Black students.[30] Students have noted that lack of knowledge about HIPs, lack of time to figure out how to access and engage in them, and prohibitive costs are the main barriers to participating in HIPs.[31] That 40% of students in the NSSE survey have not participated in at least two HIPs indicates that universities have work to do to achieve equitable excellence in education for students.[32]

The University of Texas El Paso (UTEP) Edge program makes HIPs and data-informed advising the center of the university's student success program (https://www.utep.edu/edge/). The only open-access R1 university—55.8% of students are economically disadvantaged and 82.8% are Hispanic—UTEP has seen a 63% increase in enrollment since 2000 and a 149% increase in graduations. The university has achieved a first-year retention rate (77.20%) greater than the average first-year retention rate of selective institutions (75%). UTEP took HIPs to scale. For example, previously 39% of seniors engaged in research with a faculty member—a successful but expensive model. When UTEP developed a first-year research-intensive sequence, 4-year graduation rates for students in the research-intensive first-year sequence jumped to 20% higher than those not in the sequence. In a recent study of the baccalaureate origin of Hispanic PhDs, UTEP was eighth in the country. Students perform over one million hours of service learning per year (a $29-39 million economic impact on the local economy); 67% of students in the 2019 NSSE survey reported participating in service learning.

SERVICE LEARNING

At **Duke University**, over 35 units offer nearly 200 sections of service-learning courses through Duke Service-Learning (https://servicelearning.duke.edu). More than 1,700 students enroll annually for the opportunity to take their learning into the real world, become more familiar with the surrounding community, and develop applicable problem solving, leadership, and critical thinking skills— skills that they take with them after graduation. Students at **Louisiana State University** can earn the Engaged Citizens designation by completing seven credits of service-learning courses, 100 hours of community service, and a reflective essay (https://tinyurl.com/y78je9fh). The courses allow students to put scholarship into practice, make meaningful contributions to their community, and powerfully retain course material. At **Case Western Reserve University**, Civic Engagement Scholars commit to working with a community partner for a year, engaging in direct civic engagement and meetings and reflecting in writing on their experience; the program is run through the Center for Civic Engagement and Learning (https://tinyurl.com/47c6xat2).

Making HIPs accessible can bring significant gains in student success, as the example of The University of Texas at El Paso, above, shows.

Strategies

◢ Understand who participates in evidence-based practices and HIPs and evaluate the quality of the opportunities. Participation will differ across student demographics. Some HIPs will be more impactful than others. HIPs are transformative only if they are well designed: quality requires assessment. AAC&U's publications offer useful guidance on the following: barriers to engagement for underserved students and a toolkit for assessing equity in HIPs; strategies for ensuring quality and scaling them; and the impact of HIPs, including on underserved populations.[33]

◢ Make evidence-based and high-impact practices core, not "extra." Embedding HIPs in courses can help ensure that all students experience them.[34] For example, authentic, collaborative, experiential learning opportunities within courses could feature partnership projects with local organizations in which students get practical experience while benefiting those organizations, increasing connections to the surrounding community, and developing the tools of civic engagement.

◢ Pay particular attention to those evidence-based practices and HIPs that tend to be outside the normal course schedule—such as internships and study abroad—and in which students from marginalized groups participate less frequently. The need to work makes unpaid internships, often at nonprofits, seem nonstarters, limiting students' career exploration. Study abroad—which, when well-designed, can be truly transformative—is out of reach for many. Develop attractive fundraising opportunities for named scholarships for low- and moderate-income students for internships and study abroad. Boston University's Yawkey Foundation Nonprofit Internship Program is one model (https://tinyurl.com/2dkkmnej). Offer— or connect students to universities that offer—high-quality study abroad programs that cost, all inclusive, no more than a term on campus. Michigan State University is doing so.

◢ Expand HIPs through technology. For example, enable more study abroad by offering in online format required courses not available abroad, and use digital platforms to expand collaborative projects with community partners, alumni, part-time and full-time students, as well as students and organizations abroad. Learning to use technology to develop learning modules could become a HIP in itself. Consider providing seed funding to faculty for development of, and research on, new, digitally enabled or digitally based HIPs. HIPs are well-documented but need not be fixed in physical space.

✺ Communicate the value and availability of HIPs to advisors. Advisors can alert students to their importance, can encourage students to participate, and can help them figure out how to do so.

4. Teaching: How will we ensure that our students—all of them, without exception—are educated using evidence-informed pedagogies in intentionally inclusive and empathy-based educational environments?

> We used to wash our hands with benzene because if you get something really grimy on there, it's damn good at getting it off. But it gave a bunch of people cancer. We would fire somebody if they washed their hands with benzene today. That's just as old a technique as droning on with . . . chalk in front of 200 people [and giving them] . . . high stakes multiple choice tests.
>
> – Holden Thorp, Editor, *Science*, Boyer 2030 Commissioner

> Faculty should be aware of the abundant existing research on pedagogy that will not only help students understand core concepts and research in their discipline, but also engage them in a way that helps close achievement gaps.
>
> – Barbara R. Snyder, President, Association of American Universities, Boyer 2030 Commission Co-Chair

Teaching and learning are arguably the lifeblood of institutions of higher education. U.S. research universities, their core research missions and complexity notwithstanding, are very much institutions of higher *education*. Indeed, it is not chauvinism to observe that U.S. research universities are among the largest and most diverse, most effective, and most respected institutions of higher education in the world.

That students outnumber faculty and staff combined, and that undergraduate students usually outnumber graduate, professional, and postdoctoral students combined, will come as no surprise to laypeople and university leaders alike. It should be just as unsurprising that achieving the highest quality undergraduate course work and cocurricular learning should be—must be—equal if not superior to any competing or complementary institutional priority.

The Office for Education Abroad at **Michigan State University** (MSU) provides faculty-directed programs, direct enroll options at host universities, student exchanges with international universities, and programs through affiliated organizations (https://tinyurl.com/5xe69phf). Also, program models include traditional study abroad, research abroad, international internships, and global community-engaged learning. Nontraditional program locations comprise a sizable portion of the education program, in many cases at a lower cost. A notable portion of semester opportunities abroad are available at costs that are no higher than remaining on campus for a semester. Annually, about a quarter of MSU graduates have participated in at least one education abroad program. MSU institutional research has confirmed that MSU students who study abroad, as compared with those who do not, are more likely to graduate, graduate in a shorter time period, and graduate with a higher cumulative GPA.

Research shows that students learn more and are more likely to succeed when research-proven pedagogical techniques are used and learning environments are inclusive.[35] Active learning strategies—including low-stakes or ungraded assignments enriched by instructor input, formative as well as summative assessment, and "flipping" large-enrollment classes to maximize use of class meeting time for higher-order activities such as small group discussion and group problem-solving—are among the techniques that best engage students, expand learning, and address entrenched inequities in student success.

Many faculty members use these and similar pedagogical techniques already, and some have done so, and done so effectively, for many years.[36] But these techniques are not yet a baseline standard. They are not yet taken-for-granted professional minimums. One can still walk into a classroom in which no thought has been given to inclusive pedagogy. Faculty do not routinely review one another's knowledge of germane research in pedagogy, course design, and inclusive practices. Systemic adoption of such practices remains elusive, leaving unrealized their full benefits for equity and excellence.[37]

— ✦ —

Centers for teaching and learning (CTLs) are embodying their "center" titles on U.S. college and university campuses. CTLs are critical hubs for faculty and graduate students around professional learning and community-building. In addition, CTLs take on roles as organizational change agents to move forward key institutional initiatives, particularly around student learning and success. A majority of undergraduates in the US study on a campus served by a CTL, and on campuses where CTLs are active, a majority of faculty engage with the center.

— Mary Wright, Associate Provost for Teaching and Learning, Brown University, Boyer 2030 Commissioner

Centers for teaching and learning (CTLs) have grown in number and expanded collaboration with academic units and faculty leaders. By and for instructors at all levels and oriented in usually de facto support of what the Boyer 2030 Commission calls the equity/excellence imperative, CTLs are the principal institutional repository for pedagogical expertise and the principal institutional source for professional development opportunities designed to disseminate research-based inclusive pedagogies.[38] Most instructors already use a combination of lecture and active learning.[39] Many universities offer pedagogical boot camps for new faculty, such as the University of California, Santa Cruz's New Faculty Teaching Academy (https://tinyurl.com/yt2y86as). Many although not all doctoral students receive at least some pedagogical training, benefiting their current as well as future students.[40]

— ✍ —

Doctoral education: "*That's* where you're going to get the pedagogical experience, the culturally responsive strategies that are going to engage."

— Deborah Santiago, Co-Founder and CEO, *Excelencia* in Education, Boyer 2030 Commissioner

Higher education organizations also provide opportunities for pedagogical education. AAC&U's TIDES program is taking a holistic, data-informed approach to increasing student diversity in STEM (https://tinyurl.com/ydwwebs7); and the AAU's STEM Education Initiative (https://tinyurl.com/3anncudw) and APLU's Powered by Publics Teaching and Learning efforts (https://tinyurl.com/mv78ey65) are facilitating ongoing change at hundreds of universities.

What more, then, is needed to establish evidence-based inclusive teaching practices as an institutional *norm*, that is, where their presence is an expectation and where experimentation and innovation are rewarded, and where their absence is understood as substandard, unprofessional, and thus unacceptable? The answer is three-fold:

- ✍ Leadership from presidents/chancellors, provosts, deans, chairs.
- ✍ Elevation of expertise in, and ongoing development of, evidence-based inclusive teaching practices in the faculty role, and in faculty hiring and evaluation.
- ✍ Nurturing student-centered research university campus cultures.

Strategies

✍ Elevate teaching excellence as a principal marker of institutional excellence and formally define teaching excellence, recognizing both institution-wide standards and disciplinary specifics. Definitions provide guidance for pedagogical training for graduate students, standards of evaluation for new faculty hires, and expectations for faculty development and reward.

✍ Develop holistic evaluation of teaching that includes multiple measures for promotion and tenure/job security. The

The AAU Undergraduate STEM Education Initiative, which, to date, has involved over 1,000 instructors and campus leaders in sustainable change, has found that collective department responsibility (rather than individual faculty responsibility) for introductory courses, supported by educational experts within departments, and long-term university commitment to excellent, equitable teaching were among the best strategies for achieving sustained, systemic change. Results of incorporating evidence-based teaching practices in courses on AAU member campuses include dramatic reductions in achievement gaps especially for women, underrepresented minorities, and first-generation students at some universities; widespread decreases in rates of D grades, F grades, and withdrawals from a course; increased persistence to the next or later courses and success in later courses as measured by grade performance; improved performance on exams sponsored by disciplinary societies; and stronger performance on disciplinary concept inventories.[96]

The **University of Oregon**'s provost is leading the exemplary effort through its Supporting Faculty Success program to elevate teaching excellence, define "teaching quality," and align it with "teaching development [for faculty and Ph.D. students], evaluation, and rewards systems" to create "an inclusive, engaged, and research-informed teaching culture that has the power to shape the experience of every student" (https://tinyurl.com/2ttutycx).

pitfalls of student course evaluations as primary measures of teaching are well-documented and include bias against women and racially minoritized faculty and inadequacy as measures of teaching effectiveness.[41] For annual reviews, gather more documentation of what goes into excellent teaching of excellent courses, such as time and effort spent on professional learning. The University of California, Irvine, the University of Colorado-Boulder, and the University of Kansas have undertaken exemplary reforms using different models tailored to their campuses.[42] Holistic, multimodal evaluation may use student surveys as helpful records of student experience but alongside such other measures of inclusive teaching excellence as: evaluations by trained faculty peers; documented professional development in teaching, advising, and mentoring; participation in curriculum revision, course redesign, and scholarship of teaching and learning (SOTL); and documented improvements in student learning outcomes and classroom culture. *Transforming teaching evaluation can be a powerful mechanism for increasing teaching and learning quality.*[43]

— ❦ —

If the leadership at some prominent university said, "We know these are better teaching methods. We're going to require everybody to be evaluated on how well they achieve those. We're going to hire new faculty based on their understanding and readiness to implement these in their teaching," then that would make change happen very quickly.

– Carl Wieman, Nobel Laureate, Professor of Physics and of Education, Stanford University[44]

❦   Emphasize the departmental (rather than individual faculty) responsibility for the curriculum of courses, quality of teaching, and design of assessments.[45] Departments should develop a *collective* approach to, and reputation for, teaching excellence—and be rewarded for that. Studies find that faculty's sense of peer influence and community is instrumental in shaping use of evidence-based teaching, in some instances, more important than rewards.[46]

❦   Support teaching and learning centers as sources of institutional infrastructure to help catalyze student success.[47] Administrative reporting lines notwithstanding, CTLs must be integral to undergraduate affairs and its strategy for meeting the equity/excellence imperative. To spur such development, the Howard Hughes Medical Institute's Inclusive Excellence 3 (IE3) program is providing funding to 4-year institutions to build inclusive, supportive, and effective learning communities (https://tinyurl.com/5n7kf3z6).

✦ Support university-wide expectations by providing on-going development opportunities in research-informed pedagogy for all members of the university community who teach or who will teach. Provide faculty with evidence-based resources to create equitable learning environments.[48]

5. Advising: How can we ensure that all students receive excellent advising—*holistic* advising that is student-centered and encompasses academic, career, and basic needs guidance—so students can best benefit from our complex institutions?

> Good advising may be the single most underestimated characteristic of a successful college experience.
>
> – Richard J. Light, Harvard University[49]

Advising is the dialogue that brings universities and students into focused conversation. Advisors, be they faculty or professional advising staff, are educators who educate students, not on select subject matter in a dedicated course, as course instructors do, but about curricula and degree programs as a whole, as well as the students' major fields of study, related concentrations, minor fields, and other academic undertakings. Advisors educate concerning the institution itself about its co- and extracurricular opportunities; about postgraduate opportunities, including nationally competitive scholarships, graduate and professional school programs, and, of course, career options; about adjusting to, exploring, even perhaps undertaking to challenge and change existing campus cultures and normative expectations; and so on. Advisors seek to support students' basic needs, including, crucially, mental health. This is not an exhaustive list.

Advising is undertaken by a range of university personnel: faculty; financial aid specialists; primary role advisors; student affairs staff members; diversity, equity, inclusion, and justice (DEIJ) professionals; academic coaches; mentors; trained peers; and more.

At large research universities, an advisor is often the person to whom students turn first, an anchor for support and guidance.

Organizing and sufficiently funding advising to best concentrate impact is an essential organizational challenge. Advisors want to do well by their students, but too often, advising ends up being transactional (approving a course

UTEP, an R1 Hispanic-serving institution, has increased first-year retention, completion, and postgraduate study rates. Key is focus on holistic advising with five central components: data-driven approach with academic, financial, and social risk factors available to advisors for each student; every student has a professional advisor; a strengths-based, not deficit-based perspective; immediate and persistent engagement with each student; development of academic and cocurricular pathways to degrees based on each student's interests, aspirations, and commitments. Crucially, UTEP's advising model includes cross-training of faculty and professional staff advisors. Commitment to this advising model resulted in a 4.2 percentage point increase in first-year retention rates in a pilot group over three years.

schedule, answering a routine question, lifting a registration block); too often, the purpose of advising is differently understood among advisors, leaving students unevenly served; too often for faculty, advising's role in their portfolio is under-articulated and under-rewarded; too often, advising is uncoordinated, sending students in a discouraging, sometimes defeating, search for support.

— ◆ —

As our nation works towards closing attainment gaps for low-income, first-generation and students of color, it is clear that creating institutional practices that center on holistic advising redesign is a critical step in reaching these goals. College and university leaders must address gaps in institution-wide coordination and collaboration to support students in their journey to achieve their academic, career and personal goals.

— Kevin Kruger, President, National Association of Student Personnel Administrators (NASPA), Boyer 2030 Commissioner

Yet, research on student success finds that "the quality of academic advising . . . is the single most powerful predictor of satisfaction with the campus environment for students at four-year schools."[50] Most importantly, students who express satisfaction with their academic advising and their relationship with their academic advisors are more likely to persist at their universities.[51]

Holistic advising inevitably intersects with career preparation and professional development. *Integrating Career Advising for Equitable Student Success: A Higher Education Toolkit*, published by the American Association of State Colleges and Universities, provides actionable recommendations and "checkmarks" for integrating academic and career advising as one of the most likely practices to increase student career mobility after graduation (https://tinyurl.com/3fxhjbe4).

Consistent, holistic advising is essential to addressing the equity/excellence imperative. Culturally responsive advising that creates belonging and community can also be powerful in advancing campus equity goals broadly. Research from the Advising Success Network (ASN) confirms that a well-trained advisor who can guide students as they navigate the complexity of college has a positive impact on students' overall success.[52] Coordinated by the National Association of Student Personnel Administrators (NASPA), the ASN comprises five organizations supporting institutions in holistic advising redesign to advance success for Black, Latinx, Indigenous, Asian, and Pacific Islander students and students from low-income backgrounds, and offers a trove of resources (https://www.advisingsuccessnetwork.org).

Recognition of the critical role advising plays in equitable student success and in ensuring an excellent undergraduate experience for all students has led research universities to increasingly invest in advising and, crucially, in the technology essential to scaling holistic advising. Technology can free advisors' time for the substantive guidance that only they can provide and thereby enables more students to be served more effectively. Technology can be used for answering routine questions, academic planning and auditing, managing advising caseloads and communications, sending student alerts and notifications, performance measurement and management, and such diagnostics as identifying students who might need a helping hand.

> Both my grandparents in Puerto Rico on my mother's side had gone to college, and my father's father in New York City had attended college as well. So my parents understood the value of education early on. I definitely grew up in a college-going culture and saw the difference it made in the lives of those around me. . . . I used to say Mrs. Obama was a "dream whisperer" for students. She gave them the freedom to see what they might become. That's why we called her the "school counselor in chief."
>
> – Eric Waldo, Founding Executive Director of Michelle Obama's Reach Higher, Boyer 2030 Commissioner[53]

Key to the use of technology to scale advising is highly trained advisors who can use it fully and effectively. Universities have undertaken efforts to train and support faculty and staff advisors across roles, with concomitant opportunities for promotion and pay increases. The Boyer 2030 Commission applauds universities that have invested in creating professional career tracks and professional development opportunities, including especially support for engagement in scholarship, for staff for whom academic advising is a primary responsibility. That NACADA: The Global Community for Academic Advising (https://nacada.ksu.edu) counts over 12,000 individual members reflects the professionalization of academic advising.

Georgia State University has achieved lauded gains in persistence and graduation success by, in part, coupling innovative academic advising practices with the potential of advisor-facing digital platforms to help identify otherwise difficult to assess student success issues at the individual as well as the curricular level.[97]

University leaders who have invested in reform of their advising systems—from personnel to technology to coordination to new advising practices—have seen retention and graduation rates rise and student satisfaction increase.

Strategies

◢ Provide all students with a lead advisor/mentor with whom they can develop a long-term relationship and with whom they are *required* to meet each term.

◢ Empower university-wide advising leaders—e.g., assistant provosts for and/or executive directors of advising—to manage and assess coordination, consistency, and quality of approach across advisors, and consider new organizational structures that reduce inefficient redundancies.

◢ Clearly articulate the purpose and role of advising for faculty—and make it an explicit part of evaluation for merit raises, reappointment, promotion, and tenure/job security.

◢ Integrate advising into campus DEIJ work, and train advisors accordingly. They can, in turn, train others.[54]

◢ Deploy technologies to support students, empower advisors, facilitate communication, and free advisors to personally engage students who most need it, when they need it. The Advising Success Network offers a guide to selecting, and preparing a campus to effectively use, technology to support and help scale holistic advising (https://tinyurl.com/ajjfbbj4).

Rather than multiply the number of people on campuses who are part of the student success initiative, higher education should consolidate the work of mentors, academic coaches and career counselors under one academic advising umbrella.

– Eric R. White, Executive Director emeritus,
Division of Undergraduate Studies,
Penn State University[55]

◢ Provide professional development for advisors to use advising technologies and develop other relevant skills (e.g., data analysis skills for identifying systemic student success issues).

◢ The commonly held 300:1 maximum advisor-to-student ratio for full-time primary role advisors and 30:1 for full-time faculty are no longer adequate staffing guidelines.[56] The Boyer 2030 Commission recommends that universities lower these ratios to best serve post-pandemic and increasingly diverse and complex undergraduate student populations, students whose complicated academic career options and life circumstances require more, not less, expert academic and personal guidance. Ratios will vary according to many factors and distinctive campus milieux, including the mix of duties assigned to each advisor, but 250:1 and 25:1 are realistic maximum ratios at large, complex, and academically demanding research universities. Deploying advising technology will be essential to enabling advisors at these ratios to perform the outreach and support of students required for guidance that will increase college completion. There is no doubt that this will require resources. As the examples above demonstrate and recent research by Tyton Partners confirms, however, universities with a well-designed and coordinated advising system with adequate caseloads and well-used technology have reduced equity gaps and increased student success, which should also increase revenue, reputation, and public trust.[57]

6. Faculty Rewards and Structure: How can we best recognize, support, and reward faculty across all appointment types for the expertise and dedication they bring to achieving equitable, excellent undergraduate education?

> The lack of tangible career-related returns on teaching remains the central barrier to improving it.
>
> – Jonathan Zimmerman, Judy and Howard Berkowitz Professor in Education, University of Pennsylvania[58]

The Boyer 2030 Commission heard from higher education experts, faculty, and university leaders that aligning the faculty rewards structure with the stated educational mission of the university is the most important reform we can make to ensure sustained, authentic institutional change in the quality of undergraduate education.

If such change were easy, it would have been done already, but universities *are* finding innovative and flexible ways to rethink faculty rewards for faculty across all appointment types and restructuring the faculty to advance equity and excellence in undergraduate education. Engaging departments—where standards are set and where recommendations for renewal, promotion, tenure, job security, and merit raises originate— is key to success.

Undergraduate students are taught by an ever-increasing variety of faculty members, ranging from tenure stream

INNOVATIVE ADVISING

Duke University has instituted the Academic Guides program that "integrates academic coaching and whole student support into the fabric of the Duke campus residential experience" by helping students make the connection to the right people in Duke's network of resources. The Academic Guides program works with faculty and staff in supporting students (https://academicguides.duke.edu).

EVALUATION MODELS

The dean of **Michigan State University**'s College of Arts and Letters is working with associate deans and department chairs on rethinking the merit review and the tenure and promotion processes around a framework that takes intellectual leadership as its goal. The framework encourages a move away from measuring the things that are a means to an end and instead thinking about the end, what the goals of the work ought to be, and how leaders can value these things. As a result, the faculty evaluation process has become much more individualized (https://tinyurl.com/4bma49us).[98]

faculty, to full-time lecturers, some with promotional tracks and long-term contracts, to adjuncts and part-time instructors, and others—all bringing varieties of experience, interests, and expertise that enrich the undergraduate experience. Around 70% of faculty members at all U.S. higher education institutions are non-tenure-track faculty (NTTF).[59] Many are highly dedicated and highly qualified. They believe teaching is important work and want to do well by their students. They are supported and motivated as teachers by faculty structures and rewards that provide commensurate recognition and by the educational mission of their universities.

Many teaching faculty, however, work under adverse conditions that make it difficult for them to leverage fully their expertise and participate in the life of the university to the benefit of the students and the university as a whole. While progress has been made and conditions differ across universities, many full- and part-time teaching faculty continue to experience limited influence over curriculum design and planning; last-minute hiring; lack of office space; exclusion from staff support; inequitable compensation; lack of job security, healthcare, and retirement benefits; inability to participate meaningfully in faculty governance; exclusion from or lack of support for professional development; and lack of respect from tenure-stream colleagues. Teaching professors are disproportionately women. Equity must be a goal here as well.

The effect of poor working conditions on the quality of undergraduate education is clear: increased reliance on part-time faculty, especially, is associated with decreased retention and graduation rates, decreased academic rigor and grade inflation (the result of perverse institutional pressures

A Note on Terminology

Among other difficulties, the term "non-tenure-track faculty" calls faculty by what they are not. Adrianna Kezar, Dean's Professor of Leadership, Wilbur-Kieffer Professor of Higher Education, and Director of the Pullias Center for Higher Education at the University of Southern California, observes, "There is no decided upon term to date and the academy needs one! I personally favor teaching professors. Another one I like is VITAL faculty. It stands for visitors, instructors, temporary [or TAs] and lecturers—an umbrella term."[99] To acknowledge this unsettled terrain, the Boyer 2030 Commission here uses a variety of terms, recognizing both the many contributions these faculty members make to our universities and the reality of the low status they too often occupy.

on contingent faculty), and less exposure for students to impactful pedagogical practices.[60]

> Existing research on the connections between non-tenure-track faculty working conditions and student learning show that working conditions shape the ways that faculty do their work, which in turn affects student experiences.
>
> – Pullias Center for Higher Education[61]

Institutions that align their educational mission and increase their support for VITAL faculty can expect to see increases in positive student outcomes. For university leaders contemplating how best to undertake reform of faculty structure and rewards, University of Maryland higher education scholar KerryAnn O'Meara has noted "how faculty appointment and reward systems can support distinctive institutional missions, goals and objectives, and enable a diverse faculty to flourish." Expanded thinking about the goals of reform is a place to start: "(a) improving transparency, clarity, and consistency; (b) aligning reward systems and missions; (c) expanding measures of impact; (d) improving access and equity for a more diverse faculty; (e) enhancing flexibility; and (f) strengthening accountability."[62] The Boyer 2030 Commission recommends her work and that of the University of Southern California's Pullias Center for Higher Education cited above and below.

The foregoing implies the opportunity for strategically securing and supporting the intergenerational *team* (faculty of all kinds, postdocs, graduate students, undergraduate students, and staff) as a distinctive strength of research universities.

Strategies

- Reallocate resources to support faculty, especially VITAL faculty, to meet the equity/excellence imperative. Difficult as this is, it must be done.

- Center excellence in teaching via annual reviews and promotions (and tenure when applicable) for all faculty with teaching in their portfolios. Celebrate teaching at every opportunity.

- Redesign the evaluation of teaching to include multiple forms of evidence.

- Foster a "culture of teaching" within departments/units. Recognize and reward departments, not just individuals, for their educational excellence.

NEW FACULTY MODELS

USC's Pullias Center for Higher Education's Delphi Project on the Changing Faculty and Student Success (https://pullias.usc.edu/delphi/) has been working since 2012 in partnership with AAC&U to better support part-time, contingent, and non-tenure-track faculty while helping create new faculty models for institutions of higher education to adopt. Its website contains research, case studies of new models, and useful tools to help universities better support teaching faculty for improved student outcomes (https://pullias.usc.edu/delphi/resources/). These include a realistic guide to the cost of such support, organized by changes for which few or no resources are needed to those with substantial costs requiring new or reallocated funding.

T&P STANDARDS

At **Indiana University-Purdue University Indianapolis**, a flexible set of tenure and promotion criteria for excellence in scholarship, teaching, and service has been established that takes into account different levels of contribution in different phases of a faculty career. In addition, to advance the university's diversity, equity, and inclusion (DEI) goals, it is implementing a new DEI Pathway for tenure and promotion that rewards faculty for their DEI work either as its own category or integrated with research, teaching, and service (https://tinyurl.com/34hvnk4p).[100]

Worcester Polytechnic Institute has created "a new tenure track for teaching faculty with appropriate criteria (based primarily on teaching), longer-term contracts for the remaining full-time NTTF with clear conditions for reappointment and protections against retaliation, and full inclusion in faculty governance for all secured full-time NTTF."[101] Collaboration between a faculty task force, the provost, and president was key. The **University of Denver** (DU) undertook to institutionalize "a culture of respect for teaching and professional faculty" in concert with implementing a new track of "non-tenure-track full-time faculty" with five-year "renewable contracts and pathways to promotion, a defined role in university governance and a pathway to professional advancement and formal promotion."[102] These models distinguish teaching faculty from research-active faculty who also teach. Another model is one that recognizes different phases in a faculty career and adjusts the criteria for evaluation accordingly: faculty can rotate among periods of dedication to teaching, research, and university leadership and be recognized for their service equitably.[103] The TIAA Institute publishes an ongoing series of useful reports on the faculty workforce.[104]

> Unless we work with disciplinary societies to change the culture, changing the reward structure is not going to make any difference because it's still up to one's departmental colleagues to make an initial recommendation.
>
> — Lynn Pasquerella, President, AAC&U, Boyer 2030 Commissioner

Undertake careful, intentional efforts to restructure the faculty for the future, with equity and respect for the many varied contributions of faculty an essential through-line.[63]

Align the structure of the faculty to achieve core institutional goals. Teaching, learning, and research are all central. Each university will have additional mission-based goals. Individual faculty, whose own learning and development are also a core priority, will contribute variously to these goals over time and throughout the course of evolving professional careers. Support for faculty is tantamount to support for their students, including especially their undergraduate students.

Prioritize professionalism for all faculty. This includes just compensation and benefits; meaningful inclusion in shared governance; opportunities for professional development; access to periodic, constructive evaluation; and clear pathways for meaningful advancement and promotion. Achieving this essential goal will require rethinking the de facto hierarchy of research and teaching and recognizing in practice that excellent research and excellent teaching are equally necessary to the mission of the research university and that their value must be recognized in multiple ways.

Work with faculty and faculty leaders to render pertinent challenges and opportunities transparent. Engage faculty and faculty leaders to benefit from the experience and expertise of the faculty, who, per the norms of shared governance and as a matter of common sense, know well what is needed and what will work best for their institutions.

III. Facilitating Success/Eliminating Barriers

Many marquee undergraduate student programs are designed to simultaneously facilitate success, eliminate barriers, and serve as models for the rest of campus. They will, the thinking goes, serve as the leading edge of change, as catalysts for structural and cultural change to come. Model programs showcase faculty and staff supporting students in overcoming barriers, while inspiring student success fuels changes in curricula, pedagogy, and, perhaps most importantly, in assumptions about students and their potential for success.

Some programs, like the University of Maryland, Baltimore County's Meyerhoff Scholars Program, aimed at increasing minority representation in science and engineering, have been extraordinarily successful and adapted by other universities (https://tinyurl.com/5axa65jx). Such programs, however, tend to be costly and serve only a portion of the students, and the good work they do needs to be repeated for each cohort of students. This model of change can also impose a burden on the small group of faculty and staff responsible for leading wider change. Often this burden is also felt keenly by the students these programs support, many of them from low-income and underrepresented groups, who are held up as examples of, and advocates for, doing things differently. That these students undertake this work so willingly and skillfully is a testament to their individual leadership.

What if, alternatively, universities scrutinized their histories, cultures, and structures, enhanced what works to open paths to degrees, identified the barriers, and, rather than help students over the hurdles, removed the hurdles? We can change inequities of our own making.

Collaborative national efforts for structural change to advance student success are underway. SEA Change (https://seachange.aaas.org), for example, housed in the American Association for the Advancement of Science, provides resources to member universities to center equity in existing governance and accountability structures in science, technology, engineering, mathematics, and medicine (STEMM) in order to make diversity and inclusion tenets of excellence.

7. Access and Affordability: How can we recruit and best support undergraduates from diverse communities and include them in the research universities' empowering academic programs and myriad scholarly projects aimed at advancing the quality of human experience in the US and worldwide?

Access

Dubious *U.S. News and World Report* rankings of higher education institutions incentivize selectivity for selectivity's sake,

In November 2021, the **University of California (UC) Board of Regents** voted to "continue to practice test-free admissions now and into the future." With UC as a leading example, as of that date, "more than 76% of all U.S. bachelor-degree granting institutions practice test-optional or test-blind admissions."[106]

which by definition limits access. Various additional factors also limit access to higher education, including complex application processes, application fees, and federal financial aid paperwork. Moreover, admissions criteria that rely heavily on standardized test scores—proven by research to be poor as well as biased indicators of first-year student success—and on activities outside of K–12 school records bias admissions against capable yet under-resourced prospective students. Even implicit bias among university personnel can adversely affect pursuit of equity/excellence. These are among the findings of a 2022 National Association for College Admission Counseling (NACAC)/National Association of Student Financial Aid Administrators (NASFAA) report on barriers for Black students in admissions and for underserved groups generally in financial aid award distribution.[64] The Pell awardees chart in the Introduction to this report confirms that, as a proportion of the student population, R1/R2 universities served fewer, rather than more, low-income students in 2020 than in 2010. And the news on enrolling underrepresented students is at best mixed, as the enrollment by race chart in the Introduction indicates.

Many institutions, however, are making promising changes to advance equity in college admissions. Most notably, "test optional" admissions policies, implemented of necessity during the pandemic, are continuing at a number of universities, enabling students with good scores from under-resourced or unknown high schools to distinguish themselves while mitigating the prominence of test scores in admissions decisions. Additionally, some selective institutions, such as Johns Hopkins University, are reconsidering legacy admissions as a first step in a "broader reinvestment in poor and middle-class students."[65]

Affordability

It hardly needs saying that college costs and student debt are a major factor in declining public trust in higher education. They hinder student success and college completion, and they can have long-term financial repercussions, especially for those who leave college without a degree.[66]

Three factors contributing to college costs and their consequences deserve attention:

1. Rising cost to students of tuition, room, and board, plus fees and other expenses, caused or exacerbated by declining state support and by the increased expense for universities of educating students.

2. Extended time to degree, summer courses, and over-loads drive up costs for students. These disadvantage low-income and historically minoritized students disproportionately. According to 2019 National Center for Education Statistics (NCES) data, 58% of Black and 64% of Latino students earned a degree within six years at a research university (R1 and R2), compared with nearly 73% of White students.[67] Only 21% of both low-income and first-generation dependent students first enrolling in a 2- or 4-year institution in 2011–2012 earned a bachelor's degree as they intended, compared to 66% of those who were neither low-income nor first-generation.[68]

3. Students who do not complete a degree, especially if they leave with college debt, may be worse off economically than if they never went to college, among other deleterious effects. Universities such as the University of South Florida and Georgia State University are increasing degree completion, closing the completion gap, and, not incidentally, increasing revenue.

The equity/excellence imperative requires universities to increase affordability by exercising the considerable control they have over time to degree by, again, prioritizing the support students need to complete the degree and close the completion gap and by prioritizing fundraising for financial aid.

Strategies

✶ Ensure that prospective students understand how the "cost of attendance" can differ from the "sticker price" which can have a chilling effect especially on first-generation students and those of limited means.

✶ Ensure holistic review of applications by: giving weight to demonstrated resilience, tenacity, and determination of applicants; reducing the weight of potentially biased and narrow measures; and providing regular training for admissions staff in conducting holistic reviews in ways that reduce bias.

✶ Ensure *all* admitted students are advised about the cost of the degree and what expenses financial aid will cover. "Cost of Degree" includes overloads and summer courses, all fees (including often hidden course fees), travel, books, and living expenses, in addition to tuition, room, and board.

✶ Manage cost of degree by making 4-year graduation the norm for all degrees for all full-time students, notwithstanding that some students, for good reason, may choose to take longer. Ensure that undergraduate degrees (general education + college requirements + major + electives, including all prerequisites) *can* be completed in 4 years, without overloads and summer classes, which are often not advisable or even possible for students from under-resourced high schools or for low- and middle-income students. *In describing degree programs and advising students, be transparent from the start about degree programs that take longer and their costs.*

◆ Support doubling Pell grants. In 1975–1976, the maximum Pell grant covered 79% of tuition, fees, room and board at a public institution; in 2021-22 it covered 28% (https://tinyurl.com/mv53je4m).

◆ Make fundraising for need-based aid a top priority. Consider shifting institutional aid from merit- to need-based aid.

◆ Consider setting a benchmark for reasonable total debt. Some universities set that benchmark at $20,000, while others compare reasonable total debt to that associated with the price of a midrange new car.

◆ Some universities may want to consider the role dual enrollment might play both in encouraging high school students to see themselves in college and in reducing the cost of a degree. Strengthening pathways from community colleges also achieves the same goals.

8. Degree Pathways: How can we identify the curricular and other opportunities to facilitate degree completion at our universities—and leverage and enhance them? How can we identify curricular and other similarly institutionalized barriers to degree completion—and remove them?

> As a SEISMIC scholar . . . I have learned about methods and practices that help increase a student's science identity and perseverance in STEM. This connects to my own interests as I have become more informed about the factors that play a role in helping students get into and finish STEM careers.
>
> – Paola Pantoja, undergraduate student studying mathematics and Chicano/a studies with a minor in education, University of California, Davis[69]

The Boyer 2030 Commission urges universities to continue to analyze themselves from the *students'* perspective, to better identify effective pathways as well as still-entrenched barriers to student success. Mapping the degree structure for each program—general education/core curriculum, major requirements, and, if applicable, college requirements, along with electives—is the place to start to clarify the purpose and interrelationship of requirements for students, faculty, and staff.

We already know many ways to open the pathways to degrees for our diverse students and improve the quality of their education:

- Some are curricular and pedagogical, such as: examining student pathways through degree requirements in order to identify and streamline unintended complexity and render the degree program more open to all students; reevaluating prerequisites to align them with subsequent course content or, when discovered to be unnecessary or even minimally beneficial, to eliminate them; developing effective online modules and other just-in-time supports to enable students to acquire or brush up on knowledge and skills as they need them instead of adding prerequisites; grading based on individual achievement of learning outcomes rather than on imposed class curves.
- Some are administrative, such as aligning course offerings, availability, and scheduling with degree requirements and course sequencing, key in enabling systemic student success.
- Some involve intentional development of supportive, equitable learning environments so students know that they belong and have confidence that the university they have chosen is truly there for them. This may entail faculty proactively supporting students for success, course by course, and making their students' success a measure of their own success.

We know many of the systems-level indicators of success: low DFW rates in courses, especially introductory courses; success of low-income students and students from marginalized groups equal if not superior to that of the student body as a whole; increased 4-year graduation rates for all full-time students, with no equity gap; low course overload rates; timely graduation of transfer students, with low rate of previously completed courses repeated at their graduating institutions; and low rate of student attrition due to financial struggles. Faculty must analyze and act to achieve such results.

The experience for transfer students deserves particular attention. As the National Task Force on the Transfer

ADDRESSING CURRICULAR COMPLEXITY

The **Curricular Analytics** Toolkit (https://ueru.org /curricular-analytics) enables faculty "to quantify the complexity of curricula, simulate student progress under various scenarios, and create degree plans that maximize the chances of students completing their degrees on time." Its use facilitates identifying bottlenecks in curricula, personalizing degree pathways for individual students, and creating transparent articulation pathways for transfer students. It was pioneered at the University of New Mexico and developed by Greg Heileman, vice provost of undergraduate education at the University of Arizona, and Chaouki Abdallah, executive vice president for research at the Georgia Institute of Technology.

ADVANCING SUCCESS

Excelencia in Education offers a rich array of research, resources, and opportunities for collaboration (https:// www.edexcelencia.org). In addition, the organization provides a database of programs and practices proven to work in advancing success in higher education for Latino students (https://tinyurl.com /y8d8797e).

University of South Florida's approach to college completion and closing the completion gap involves identifying those most at risk and providing holistic support. In part through a combination of structural reorganization to coordinate the work of different divisions, using analytics to identify students who could use a hand, encouraging students to seek help and faculty and staff to help remove barriers, and creating wraparound services to support students, USF has increased its 4-year graduation rate 33 percentage points since 2009.[107]

and Award of Credit pointed out in its 2021 report, 33% of the 2.8 million first-time undergraduates enrolled in fall 2011 transferred to another institution within the next six years. Articulation agreements with community colleges are demonstrated to guide students' choice of courses at their initial institution and to clarify a path to transfer that enables students to graduate within four years and within their college budget. Furthermore, timely evaluation and standardized but flexible and well-articulated approaches to faculty evaluation of credits for transfer enable students to receive credit for prior study *and* fulfill the learning outcomes of the institutions from which they seek to graduate. Currently, 22% of credits on average do not count for transfers from 2- to 4-year institutions. Repeated courses and lengthened time to degree and, hence, increased cost are common, as are lengthy waits for transfer evaluation, making it difficult for transfer students to make informed decisions, adding alienating uncertainty to the process, and sometimes adding unexpected additional time and costs to degrees.[70]

Additionally, the Task Force's report shines light on the experience of low-income and racial minority students:

> For decades, research on transfer rates has shown a large and persistent gap between racial minority students and other student groups who transfer to a university to complete the baccalaureate degree. . . . [Student] equity gaps have failed to budge over time, raising questions about the effectiveness of existing transfer policies and practices.[71]

Equity gaps may be exacerbated by COVID-19, as students from all groups step out of community college or drop out of higher education altogether. In addition to the COVID-induced financial hardships suffered by many students transferring from community colleges to research universities, "institutions need to recognize that future transfer students may bring with them courses on their transcripts that were impacted by COVID-19 accommodations; these students should not be at a disadvantage in the transfer admission or credit award process as a result."[72]

Building on what we know about how best to open pathways to degrees can be a cost-effective way of expanding and scaling equity/excellence. Doing so, however, requires thoughtful planning, which needs available time for faculty and staff to gather information, analyze, reflect, and act.

Strategies

- Use a pathway approach to help students (including transfer students) navigate the complex matrices of requirements and prerequisites.

- Reward degree programs that implement clear pathways that enable students to complete the degree in four years and that increase completion rates and reduce equity gaps.

- Provide disaggregated student pathway data by degree program to faculty to analyze and make changes for equity and success based on analysis. "Weed-out courses," courses with high DFW rates, complex prerequisite sequences, and high-requirement majors with the expectation of overloads, summer courses and sometimes additional terms all promote "self-selection" that masks deeper forms of discrimination, among other barriers to excellent education.

- Make "cost of degree" a consideration in intentional and clear pathways to degrees.

- Make enrollment management at the course level a priority. Provide sufficient spaces in necessary courses that are offered frequently enough for all students to move through their degrees in a timely manner. Identify and address bottleneck courses, consider the full range of needs of students (e.g., those who work), and schedule courses for flexibility. Enrollment management for equity and excellence involves tracking and tackling the difficult issues of teaching loads and under-enrolled courses.

- Remove the barriers to approving transfer credit from 2- and 4-year institutions. Consider articulation agreements, a repository of approved transfer courses, a central system for timely evaluation of courses, and a transparent general education program for transfer students to enable them to make a seamless transition to an affordable program at a university that is a good fit.

- Identify how resource allocation policies and practices can support (and not unintentionally limit) students' engagement in a full range of curricular and cocurricular activities.

- Identify, engage, and assist students who stopped-out to return and complete their degree programs. The Institute for Higher Education's 2022 report, *Lighting the Path*, documents how close some students are to finishing a degree and proposes strategies for reaching out and helping them over the finish line.[73]

- Fundraise and advocate to increase local, state, foundation, and private need-based aid.

9. Digital Technology: How can we use technology strategically and in financially sustainable ways to ambitiously scale up equity/excellence in undergraduate education?

> Technology is really the tool we have today to be transformative at scale.
>
> — Peter McPherson, President, APLU,
> Boyer 2030 Commission Co-Chair

> Can we conceive, prioritize, and invest in equitable undergraduate student achievement? The answer is yes, but not without the introduction of innovations and technologies that assist the breadth of the learning modalities required by a population as diverse as that of the United States.
>
> — Michael Crow, President, Arizona State University,
> Boyer 2030 Commissioner

Digital technologies are essential components for effective strategic transformation guided by the equity/excellence imperative. Some of the most promising applications of technology include academic advising, just-in-time flexible learning, and analytic tools that render visible institutionalized barriers to equity/excellence (see below for examples). Such digital innovations are an "enterprise-level" concern that requires consideration at the most senior and strategic levels as well as the broad involvement of university communities in planning, implementation, and use. In this section, we highlight university consortia and leading-edge institutions that are exemplary in their digital innovation experimentation.

There are two caveats. First, technology must never, even inadvertently, *determine* academic policy and practice, even if technologies inevitably shape them. Technologies are, by definition, means rather than ends. As Tiffany Mfume, assistant vice president for student success and retention at Morgan State University, has pointed out, "Technology shouldn't dictate the strategies, strategies should dictate the technology." She added, perhaps ruefully, "You only need [faculty, staff, student] 'buy-in' when something that took one click before now takes four clicks; something that took four clicks that now takes one—everyone says: 'how did we ever live without this?'" Second, be careful about what technology providers do with the data you provide them: some make their profits through extraction and use of data, some of it sensitive, from our institutions.

Members of the University Innovation Alliance (https://theuia.org) deserve special acknowledgment for helping to pioneer collaboration among research universities around data-informed, technologically sophisticated innovation on behalf of equity and excellence goals. Arizona State University (ASU) has used digital technologies in myriad ways, from AI-driven chatbots that make student-friendly answers to FAQs accessible (https://theuia.org/project/chatbots), to self-paced online degree programs that require mastery of rigorous learning objectives at each step in a transparent, flexible, and accessible course of study (https://asuonline.asu.edu). ASU President Michael Crow leads his university toward and advocates broadly for a focus on "digital systems that enhance the chances of success for students from a broad spectrum of our society."[74] The Boyer 2030 Commission highly recommends attention to these and all similar UIA digital innovations.

— ◆ —

We amplify what we do through technology. We have 5,600 faculty and 25,000 support staff. Teaching, learning, discovery was previously concentrated on campus. Through our technology partners, we are able to evolve the university as more than just a place, but a force to project outward. We have five times the graduates than a few years ago, and fifty times the learners. Using technology helps us do what we do.

— Michael Crow, President, Arizona State University,
Boyer 2030 Commissioner[75]

APLU's Powered by Publics initiative is a consortium of 125 change-ready universities (https://tinyurl.com/mptwu3y8) that supports use of Curricular Analytics in its Western Land-Grant and Big Ten Clusters (https://tinyurl.com/zsezadxh). In addition to enabling faculty to see the complexity of their degrees, to identify unintended roadblocks and bottlenecks, and thereby to design degrees and chart pathways that facilitate student success, as discussed above, Curricular Analytics promotes reform that helps students integrate HIPs into a 4-year course of study. Implications for the equity/excellence imperative are so great that Ascendium Education Group invested nearly $2M in UERU-headed support of further study among public

ADVANCING EQUITY/
EXCELLENCE

EDUCAUSE (https://www
.educause.edu/about) is a
nonprofit association dedicated to improving higher education through information technology. It offers a useful planning guide that, for example, advises an institutional process of developing a vision first, then understanding student success and institutional success, and finally using technology to control costs at scale.[108]

Georgia State University's technology-enabled approach to student success led to the creation of the National Institute for Student Success at Georgia State University (https://niss.gsu.edu) that "helps colleges and universities identify and resolve institutional barriers to equity and college completion by increasing their capacity to implement proven student-success systems and data-driven interventions, and enact systemic change to institutional processes and structures."

and private research universities (https://ueru.org/curricular-analytics). The Boyer 2030 Commission recommends attention to analytics that highlight institutionalized barriers to progress toward degree and completion, such as are embedded in curricular structure, and that facilitate faculty engagement in evaluating possible structural change. As Beth McMurtrie, a senior writer for *The Chronicle of Higher Education*, reports:

One of the developers of Curricular Analytics, Hayden Free, was an undergraduate studying computer-science engineering at the University of Kentucky when [he was hired] . . . to assist with programming. [Free] . . . wants professors to understand that while curricular complexity may seem like a badge of honor within a discipline, it can have life-altering and unintended consequences. "That one prerequisite might be enough to set a student back for a term," he says. "And for a student like me, first generation and on a four-year scholarship, to add an extra term has the potential to be a dream-killer."[76]

Strategies

⬤ Use digital technologies to analyze and scale to achieve equity/excellence. Develop strategies and involve end users *before* technologies are adopted and nurture campus cultures that facilitate perpetual technological innovation rather than implicitly resist it in fits and starts. In this way, universities can expand access and support equitable undergraduate student success while also benefiting from shared governance in support of systematically strengthened programs.

⬤ Consider the university's responsibility to partner with platforms that operate responsibly, are transparently governed, and do not serve as new points of resource extraction for company profit.

IV. Fostering Belonging and Equitable Campus Cultures

We catch them on the social side, the academic side, spiritual side, the cultural side. All of the entities—faculty, staff—come together to catch them early to make sure that every aspect of their life [is part of their education]. . . . Where they live, the kinds of things we expose them to, activities on campus. So we fully wrap around that cultural experience.

– Alicia Simon, General Education Faculty Curriculum
Coordinator, Clark Atlanta University

Research universities that are also historically Black colleges and universities (HBCUs) have had remarkable success in educating and graduating students of color into fulfilling lives of distinguished leadership in their workplaces and communities. Many of the aspects of campus culture that the HBCUs attend to so assiduously foster students' sense of belonging and well-being and contribute to mental health, concerns about which, needless to say, were building before the pandemic and are paramount today.

10. Nurturing Mental Health and Well-Being: How can we urgently support belonging and wellness in the university community? How can we identify and eliminate policies or practices that exacerbate mental health problems, which disproportionately affect students from underrepresented groups?

> Through increased training across departments at our colleges and universities, or simply through a little moral courage, people on our campuses can have intricate conversations to improve students' lives— emotionally, interpersonally and spiritually. It's likely that, in organic ways, such conversations would lead to greater awareness about how some prevailing mind-sets may link to the stress and distress of our students.
>
> – Gary Glass, Director of Counseling and Career Services at Oxford College, Emory University[77]

University presidents/chancellors increasingly identify student mental health as their top concern, with faculty and staff mental health trailing not far behind.[78] What's more, status quo remedies are increasingly overwhelmed by the prevalence of mental health challenges so widespread as to defy credulity.[79] Research universities—characteristically large and diverse and often experienced more as small cities than small towns—are especially challenged to nurture living and learning environments that support wellness and equitable undergraduate success. According to a 2013 report by the National Alliance on Mental Illness, two thirds of students who leave college do so because of mental health issues.[80]

Mental health and wellness are complex matters for students, faculty, and staff alike, with types of issues and levels of severity varying. Moreover, many of the sources of anxiety—the leading presenting issue in counseling—are exacerbated by academic practices like high-stakes exams

Prairie View A&M University conducts a monthly student survey around a number of domains, including food insecurity, mental health, and academic support, in order to make real-time adjustments. As surveys come in, units reach out to students to find out what's needed and to support them.

and first-year grading policies and by academic cultures that, for example, value the appearance of "effortless perfection," which Gary Glass has reported on. As Glass noted, Duke University and the University of Texas at Austin are among those that have tackled the "effortless perfection" phenomenon.[81] Meanwhile, the Massachusetts Institute of Technology (MIT) is renowned for its first-year grading policy designed to enhance *equitable learning*, not grade-induced anxiety (https://tinyurl.com/2eu5d6tk).

The excellent 2021 National Academies of Sciences, Engineering, and Medicine report on student support finds that "the stigma of mental illness is particularly powerful" for students from underrepresented groups who already "face additional challenges and stress."[82] Wake Forest University's Vice President for Diversity and Inclusion and Chief Diversity Officer José Villalba has emphasized the added burdens these mental health challenges foist upon the systemically harmed and the need for special attention not only to students who are undocumented, international, and LGBTQ+ but also to lower-paid and less secure frontline professional staff.[83]

A crisis as multifaceted as this, with more roots outside of campus life than in, calls for a both/and approach; that is, it requires efforts to address the most acute and urgent individual and group needs coupled with scaffolded institutional and cultural change that will benefit all, including faculty and staff. The latter requires widespread input and candid reflection, willingness to change, and time for experimentation.

Perhaps most importantly, we must examine institutionalized academic practices and entrenched campus cultures to assess whether they contribute to learning and well-being or, unintentionally, are themselves part of the problem. The COVID-19 pandemic revealed higher education's capacity for adaptation and change. From discontinuing use of inequitable standardized testing for admissions to reform of inequitable high-stress course designs and learning evaluation practices, the Boyer 2030 Commission urgently recommends that universities build upon what has been learned during the pandemic and continue thoroughgoing review and reform of university policies, practices, and campus cultures to promote mental health and wellness for all. University leaders can seed conversations by pointing to those who have addressed sacred cows such as the SAT/ACT and first-year course grades. That MIT retained the first and helped pioneer the second is suggestive of how each institution must discern its own distinctive mix of actions. But act we must.

Strategies

A number of promising practices and efforts are underway to promote wellness across the campus community and to respond to mental health issues:

⚡ When then–University of Cincinnati President and current University of Michigan President Santa Ono publicly shared that he had twice attempted suicide, his courageous candor helped destigmatize and focus discussion of the most urgent mental health concerns on his campus and beyond.[84] University leaders should similarly consider how they might help destigmatize seeking help for mental health challenges in their campus communities.

⚡ To address urgent as well as endemic mental health concerns in ways that strengthen large and diverse university communities, provide learning and leadership opportunities for undergraduate students, and are cost-effective, the Boyer 2030 Commission recommends peer-to-peer programs such as the Big Red Resilience Coaches at the University of Nebraska-Lincoln, where specially trained "student volunteers . . . help other students thrive and create the life they want to live, both now and in the future" (https://tinyurl.com/4kf482cz) by promoting 10 dimensions of well-being (https://tinyurl.com/zh8jtxha).

⚡ Population-wide strategies integrate well-being into the student experience. For example, the Be REAL program at the University of Washington encourages student well-being by providing "participants with opportunities to learn stress management skills, improve attention and focus, and discuss how these skills apply to daily life." Crucially, faculty and staff participate in training students, and the latter report being helped as well (https://tinyurl.com/53b7xrmr). The Ohio State University's Vice President for Health Promotion, University Chief Wellness Officer, and Professor and Dean of the College of Nursing, Bernadette Melnyk, sees opportunity to embed wellness expertise and services in academic units as well as in the university's strategic plan and in its outreach beyond campus. The Wellbeing Collaborative at Wake Forest University (https://tinyurl.com/2bfjdtpd) advances equity on college campuses through national data collection and assessment and development of evidence-based tools and programming to support community wellness. Its work focuses on four core dimensions: Meaning, Purpose, Belonging, and Engagement (https://tinyurl.com/yc868z7z). The Boyer 2030 Commission recommends programs that nurture multifaceted community relationships.

⌐ The University of Texas at Austin's SHIFT program addresses student substance abuse, a critical factor in student wellness, by providing faculty and staff knowledge and skills, as well as confidence to talk with students about mental health and substance use (https://shift.utexas.edu). Empathy for the whole student is implicit.

⌐ UC Davis established the Aggie Compass Basic Needs Center. Chancellor and Boyer 2030 Commissioner Gary May explains:

> Early in my tenure I established a series of basic needs task forces, including one on mental health care. The recommendations from that task force resulted in my establishing the Aggie Compass Basic Needs Center. In addition to sharing counseling, self-care, confidential and crisis resources in my messages to our campus community, I have never turned down a meeting with a student. Whether they email the office, make a phone call, or approach me in person, they will get a response and they can ask for a meeting. It's important that students feel they are seen, heard and represented; that they can connect with and share their concerns with campus leaders. If a student feels uncomfortable reaching out directly, I also have two undergraduate student advisors and a graduate student advisor they can contact. Our campus leaders really enjoy talking to students and having an opportunity to hear what they think, and also to see what we can do. Many of us are former student leaders and student activists ourselves, and that informs our desire to make sure we are accessible.

V. Leading Change

The scope and urgency of the change needed require leadership from the very top: presidents/chancellors and provosts leading undergraduate vice provosts/presidents and those with whom they collaborate across the university, empowering department chairs and faculty for lasting improvements.

The change called for in this report goes beyond the idea that diversifying the community of students, faculty, and staff will lead to equity and inclusion. Institutional structures need to change. Resources must be reallocated and difficult decisions made about what can no longer be done. These changes require the resolve, power, perspective, and vision that only senior leadership can provide.

That said, faculty and staff will be the heart of change. Sustained change will come from empowering them to work with their department/unit colleagues and leaders or in cross-department groups to analyze problems and develop proposed solutions.

Achieving excellence, equity, and world readiness implies changes in culture—changes, large and small, often to long-standing, sometimes cherished, mindsets and practices. Tradition binds community, and we should not underestimate the difficulty of altering or giving up what has been known and relied upon, even for a good reason. Understanding and publicly acknowledging the difficulty, along with articulated resolve, can help effect change.

Different institutional cultures, different histories, different budgetary pressures day to day and year to year, different leadership styles: all will shape how each institution develops a roadmap for meeting the equity-excellence imperative. But a roadmap must be developed. Significant change in undergraduate education can't wait.

11. Assessment and Accountability: How can we most effectively assess our progress toward meeting the equity/excellence imperative? How should we hold ourselves accountable?

The data we have been using to measure excellence in undergraduate education are no longer adequate to today's students and to a definition of excellence with a precondition of equity. To assess progress and hold ourselves accountable, we must begin by revising the metrics we use. Those new metrics, in turn, will indicate a rededication to the mission of excellent education for as broad a segment of society as possible, a mission to which research universities themselves will be held accountable and by which they will be judged.

To assess progress on the equity/excellent imperative within and among institutions and to ensure data measure what matters to fulfilling our educational missions, the Boyer 2030 Commission recommends the following:

⚬ Remove admissions selectivity as a meaningful data point, as called for in the 2022 report by NACAC and NASFAA.

⚬ Update the current metrics used on research university campuses—and insist that agencies that collect data do the same. Supporting the College Transparency Act[85] and pressing NCES to disaggregate Pell numbers demographically in IPEDS are good first steps toward the latter.

⚬ Count success metrics for *all* students, including first-year *and* transfer students, entering in *all* terms, not just fall. One example of the importance of this is that about one third of Latinx PhDs started at community colleges; our data must record their pathway and count their success.

⚬ Track student success demographically, including by low-income and first-generation status (with a shared definition), with the goal of success levels by group equal to success levels by aggregate. "Success" includes closing the equity gap in completion rates.

⚬ Track completion rates, rather than graduation rates— i.e., count all students who complete a baccalaureate degree, including those who finish elsewhere. Students who find a pathway to a degree at an institution that best suits them—perhaps with our help—are a success, not a failure.

⚬ Track graduate school and job placements at, say, 6 months and 5 years after graduation for both first-year entry and students who transferred in.

⚬ Consider different populations of undergraduates (e.g., traditional/non-traditional, full-time/part-time, first-time/transfer) and consider where different metrics of success are needed. For example, time-to-degree matters for a number of reasons, but how that measure features in "success" for the institution and for the student would differ for part-time and full-time students.

⚬ Look behind and beyond completion rates to measure equitable excellence. Meaningful data could include: participation in HIPs, as recorded by the NSSE, for example;

assessment of general education programs/education for world readiness; survey of students, say, 5, 10 and 20 years after graduation to gauge how they are making meaning of their education and what they most value about it and to gather information on job, civic engagement, and life satisfaction.

- Develop an institutional dashboard of these measures to track progress.

Assessment of institutions themselves must include measures, qualitative and quantitative, of progress on the equity/excellence imperative.

Strategies for Presidents/Chancellors and Provosts

- Communicate the message that excellent undergraduate education is a central mission of the research university. Articulate and support the short- and long-term value of undergraduate education, including and beyond immediate economic measures: transformative education for world readiness, which is preparation for work, life, and civic engagement immediately after college and over a lifetime.

- Develop a plan for equitable student and institutional success that is data-informed.

  - Update types of data collected.

  - Connect sources of data that exist in different parts of the institution. Integrate the data to meet goals.

  - Develop a student success data plan that is built on campus conversations about how to assess whether all students are equitably accessing educational opportunities and how to use that information to make necessary changes. Set meaningful and ambitious targets for the institution and hold relevant units accountable for their roles in ensuring equitable student success.

  - Continuously look at data, share the data, and implement changes informed by the data.

- Be inclusive in these reforms. Leverage the power of faculty—who will be implementing change—by empowering departments in rethinking education for excellence and equity. Involve students in change efforts and leverage the new ways of thinking and fresh insights they bring to the table. Rely on the expertise of support units such as centers for teaching and learning and institutional research offices to help develop key parts of campus plans.

*   Begin and carry through on an intentional process to restructure the faculty for excellence and equity in undergraduate education. Consider the full range of faculty appointments that can be used to hire the team of talent needed within departments to attend to both educational and scholarly responsibilities. Such a process requires leadership and supported from those at the top and must be carried out in close collaboration with the faculty governance system. The end, however, cannot be in question: a more equitable faculty structure better aligned with the university's educational mission.

*   Institutionalize equity and excellence in undergraduate education through hiring practices in order to change the traditional departmental structures that mitigate against teaching in university-wide programs such as general education and nondepartmental interdisciplinary courses. For example, at Purdue University, new tenure-track hires in the College of Liberal Arts must commit half of their teaching to the Cornerstone program described above. As you approve hires and/or work with deans, departments, and faculty to set priorities and criteria for hiring, you have the opportunity and the power to break open the silos of departments in service to *university* mission.

*   Ensure excellence in teaching when considering promotion and tenure cases. As the final or sometimes penultimate decision-makers, provosts and presidents/chancellors can lead the way within an institution in setting teaching as a real standard of excellence, a standard of excellence that has the advantage of already existing, even if not exercised to its fullest. Assert the value of teaching and ensure it is rewarded throughout a faculty member's career by communicating to departments and colleges clearly and repeatedly the importance teaching should hold in merit raises. Work with department chairs and faculty members to define the parameters of "teaching" and to institute evaluations of teaching that are as comprehensive as evaluations of research. Involve department chairs and faculty early on to develop, if necessary, the processes by which teaching could take its place beside research in evaluation. Either solely or in concert with other presidents/chancellors and provosts, bring disciplinary associations into discussion about teaching and its evaluation. Again, as Nobel Laureate and Professor of Physics and of Education at Stanford University Carl Wieman noted, "if the leadership at some prominent university said, 'We know these are better teaching methods.

We're going to require everybody to be evaluated on how well they achieve those. We're going to hire new faculty based on their understanding and readiness to implement these in their teaching,' then that would make change happen very quickly."[86]

⦁ Work with boards, state system leaders, accrediting bodies, policy makers, and public officials to create meaningful standards and measures of progress that will motivate the setting of helpful institutional priorities and guide senior leaders in achieving excellence and equity.

⦁ Collaborate with other universities on cross-institutional reforms—to share expertise and ideas, speed reform, apply for implementation grants, and leverage shared resources.

Strategies for Undergraduate Vice Provosts/Presidents[87]

⦁ Build collaborative relationships across units, as they are as important as cohesive and coordinated academic affairs teams.

◌ Quality undergraduate education is coproduced and supported by academic affairs, student affairs, enrollment management, institutional research, and diversity, equity, inclusion, and social justice professionals—indeed, by all faculty, staff, and students, the last including postdoctoral, graduate, and undergraduate. Undergraduate vice provosts/presidents (UVPs) are often called to organize university-wide collaborative groups to consistently achieve university-wide standards of quality and meet university strategic goals. Embrace this responsibility and work regularly to form university-wide coalitions that benefit from diverse perspectives and eschew bias. Wed strategy and daily practice.

◌ The 1998 Boyer Report called for a "student-centered research university."[88] From students' perspectives, divisions and reporting lines matter little if at all. View your work from a student's perspective and take that perspective to heart. Consult students and their families. Attend to generalized impressions as much as to concrete individual experiences.

⦁ Engage departments, the locus of many faculty, staff, and students' lives, as important allies in curricular change.[89] Bring them into relation with the other coproducers of undergraduate education.

♦ Student success goals measured quantitatively and student learning goals measured qualitatively are of equal and mutually reinforcing importance. Attend to both equally.

- First-to-second-year retention and 4- and 6-year graduation rates, disaggregated demographically, can be key indicators of overall program effectiveness and fairness. They are not, however, goals. They are broad indicators of systems functioning. Maintain steady focus on genuine *educational* goals, such as cultivation of world readiness.

- Embrace data-informed analysis, such as via Curricular Analytics. Share information wisely and widely so that those positioned to act can do so efficiently and effectively.

- Nurture integration of HIPs into student journeys but attend to their quality and clearly communicate their meaning and value; it's not a race to see how many HIPs students undertake. In this regard and in others, encourage sharing of insight from faculty and staff. Don't neglect local solutions to local challenges when this strategy makes good sense.

- Attention to general education/core curricula, inclusive pedagogy, HIPs, honors/scholars programs, and nationally competitive scholarships is no less or no more important than partnering with career services, attending to academic policies and practices, looking after honor and integrity practices, and similar responsibilities. Develop a holistic vision for undergraduate education that maps relationships and communicate it to others.

— ♦ —

UVPs, *use* your position—your expert on-the-ground knowledge and strategic perspective—to educate and influence those above you.

— Elizabeth Loizeaux, Boston University, former president of UERU, Boyer 2030 Commissioner ex officio

- Ideally, UVPs should advocate for the inherent simultaneity of equity/excellence, helping colleagues, for example, see summer bridge programs as nurturing student leadership excellence and honors programs as sites for expanding opportunity and broadening definitions of excellence. UVPs must interrogate false trade-offs and articulate a vision of 21st century research universities free from the harmful constraints of institutionalized barriers and campus cultures that are parochial and un-welcoming.

- Professional development is essential.
    - UVPs should encourage team-building and professional development for university-wide teams. Especially useful areas of focus are change management and equity work.

    - In addition to developing expertise in areas that often depend directly upon UVPs for leadership (e.g., academic advising, general education/core curriculum, pedagogy, etc.), UVPs should educate themselves concerning graduate education, enrollment management, advancement, shared governance, community engagement, and so forth and involve themselves in these areas when opportunities arise. Such involvement can have positive consequences for the development of undergraduate programs—where, for example, graduate students often play instructional roles and where student success is significantly impacted by financial aid and scholarship policy and fundraising can help spur innovation. But such involvement is also a prerequisite for UVPs who wish to undertake broader responsibilities in university leadership. UVPs and their colleagues should also look for opportunities to learn from and with one another, including cross-institutionally, where generous colleagues at similar institutions are available to share experience and expertise.

Strategies for Boards

Boards have an oversight and fiduciary role, not a management role in the institution, and in that context, boards should:

- Recruit, retain, and support presidents/chancellors who prioritize undergraduate education and who understand the opportunities as well as the challenges posed by pursuit of the equity/excellence imperative within research university contexts. Then give them the support and authority they need to work with faculty, staff, and students to accomplish the goals they were hired to pursue.

- Support interrogation of success metrics for what they may inadvertently conceal about equitable student outcomes; support metrics that better measure equitable student success.

    *   Support investment in equity/excellence and expect return on investment in universities better positioned to fulfill 21st century missions and generate net revenue in 21st-century environments.

    *   Support institutional reform that aims to render systemic equity/excellence in all facets of university structure, policy, and sanctioned practices. Celebrate education for world readiness and inclusive university cultures. Advocate for the public good in undergraduate education. Nurture freedom of speech and expression in conjunction with trustful campus cultures.

    *   Support collaboration between and among research universities to foster joint research and shared learning and to help lead across-the-board reform of U.S. higher education.

Conclusion

Reports of higher education's inability to change are, like Mark Twain's reported demise, greatly exaggerated. Far from the medieval cloister conjured in jest, the research university is a distinctly *modern* institution, deriving from the same social and cultural forces that produced modern science and democracy; enlivened by the universal values of liberty and equality; and, whether public or private, dedicated to a global public good. As to any sort of inflexible DNA, the response to the COVID-19 pandemic, if nothing else, demonstrates undeniably that U.S. research universities, like their respected peers worldwide, can and in fact *have* changed, and with remarkable alacrity and agility as well as sacrifice, to meet extraordinary and urgent challenges.

The Boyer 2030 Commission calls on U.S. research universities to pursue the equity/excellence imperative with the same skill and dedication, the same resilience and determination, that they mustered in facing down the challenges posed by the pandemic. It is time to seize an historic opportunity to double down in pursuit of fundamental change, to achieve equity/excellence, and to do so aware of the inequalities characteristic of higher education itself and thus in a full spirit of collaboration, sharing, and mutual aid within and among universities, for their own and for the public good, for the betterment of society, for the furtherance of the U.S. university's historical commitment to educating for a free and equitable democracy. Returning to Twain, who wrote that "it is noble to teach oneself, but still nobler to teach others—and less trouble," the Boyer 2030 Commission recommends embracing transformation before myriad exigencies demand it.

Acknowledgments

The Boyer 2030 Report was commissioned and supported by the Association for Undergraduate Education at Research Universities (UERU). The Commission wants to express its gratitude to Steven Dandaneau, executive director of UERU and associate provost at Colorado State University, who shaped this report in so many ways, and to Liz Bennett, associate director of UERU, who staffed the Commission. Thanks also go to Colorado State University, which hosts UERU, and to UERU staff member Mariah Pursley for their support. Special thanks go to UERU's core constituency, the UVPs at U.S. research universities, who helped set the priorities of this report at the start and contributed their experience and expertise throughout.

The Commission is most grateful to the staffs of the Association of American Universities (AAU) and the Association of Public and Land-grant Universities (APLU), especially Emily Miller, deputy vice president of AAU; Kacy Redd, associate vice president of APLU; and Ken Goldstein, senior vice president of AAU, who contributed so much to both the process and substance of this report.

The Commission also thanks Elizabeth Loizeaux of Boston University, former president of UERU and *ex officio* member of the commission, who wrote the report with the aid of those thanked in the previous paragraphs, especially Steven Dandaneau, Emily Miller, and Kacy Redd. Research Assistant Elizabeth Wasden of the University of Maryland, College Park provided excellent writing, editing, and research support. Karen Peirce went above and beyond in her careful copy editing of the final manuscript.

Many thanks to John Gravdahl of Colorado State University who designed the report's graphics and to Mike Palmquist of Colorado State University and the WAC Clearinghouse for the report's overall print and digital design. Both have honored Boyer 2030's history by incorporating elements of Milton Glaser's design for the 1998 Boyer Report.

The Commission is indebted to the many faculty and staff members whose research and expertise inform the report and whose willingness to consult with the Commission displays the collegiality and generosity of our universities at their best. A very special thanks to the experts listed in Appendix D who graciously gave their time to participate in information sessions exploring key areas of interest to the Commission.

The Commission's work could not have happened without the generous support of the Raikes Foundation and the Suder Foundation. Thanks to them for seeing the impact this report could have in advancing equity and excellence and for their confidence in the Commission itself.

Finally, thanks to the Commission's co-chairs, Barbara R. Snyder, president of AAU, and Peter McPherson, president of APLU, who pushed, pulled, and coaxed into being an "achievable vision" for equity/excellence in undergraduate education at our research universities.

Notes

1 The National Center for Education Statistics' (NCES) Integrated Postsecondary Education Data System (IPEDS) does not disaggregate Federal Pell Grant recipients by demographic characteristics. This does not aid, and arguably significantly hinders, pursuit of equitable student success.

2 Seventy-eight percent of doctoral universities now have a center for teaching and learning, which includes 94% of doctoral universities with very high research activity and 83% of those with high research activity, according to forthcoming research (2023) by Mary Wright, associate provost for teaching and learning at Brown University and Boyer 2030 commissioner. When the original Boyer Commission assessed the progress on its agenda in a 2001 follow-up report, it noted "considerable headway," especially in engaging undergraduates in research, reforming general education with greater emphasis on writing and math, and creating freshman seminars (p. 2).

3 National Survey of Student Engagement (2019), p. 12.

4 Davidson (2017), p. 14.

5 The Morrill Act (1862), See also Gavazzi & Gee (2018).

6 Association of American Colleges and Universities (2020), p. 8.

7 Delbanco (2022), p. 39.

8 Association of American Colleges and Universities (2020), p. 23.

9 Montás (2022)

10 As cited in Thorp & Goldstein (2018), p. 15.

11 Davidson (2017), p. 12.

12 Fischman & Gardner (2022b). See also Fischman & Gardner (2022a).

13 Hart Research Associates (2018).

14 Between 2012 and 2018, the number of majors in the largest humanities fields fell 25–30%, and evidence from individual disciplines suggests further declines since then (The Humanities Indicators Project, 2021).

One-pagers or infographics like those made by 4Humanities (https://tinyurl.com/5fh99auc) can be used to help universities and others make the case for the importance of the humanities today.

15 As cited in the Commission on the Humanities and Social Sciences (2013), p. 44.

16 Thorp & Goldstein (2018), p. 122

17 In a recent Association of American Universities public opinion poll (April 2022), 66% of the 4018 respondents, across political parties and demographic groups, said "preparing students for future careers" should be an important priority for colleges and universities. The third most frequently named problem with leading research universities, however, was "poor job preparation" (29%). While 65% found the assertion that leading research universities "effectively prepare graduates for the workforce" either "believable" or "very believable," answers were split 46% and 19%, respectively, indicating uncertainty about the extent to which this goal of undergraduate education is actually achieved.

18 Matthew T. Hora's (2016) research finds that the "skills gap" narrative, which, in the wake of the 2008 recession in Wisconsin and elsewhere, drove to prominence the idea that higher education needed to focus on immediate-need technical skills, not liberal arts, was much more nuanced and less of a gap than commonly thought. He found significant common ground between educators (including in technical colleges) and employers on the need for the habits of mind cultivated by liberal education. The AAC&U/Hanover Research surveys of employers provide useful guidance on the specifics of what employers value most and where they see college graduates well- and underprepared. See the 2020 results at Finley (2021). See also Pasquerella (2022, p. 106).

19 Cited in Commission on the Humanities and Social Sciences (2013), p. 34.

20 Jaschik & Lederman (2022).

21 For example, Virginia Tech is embedding "bridge experiences" to pave the way to first jobs and has begun developing necessary data to track the relationship between those experiences and "first destination." https://tinyurl .com/2p82vabf.

22 Fitzpatrick (2019), p. 235.

23 A Knight Foundation-Ipsos (2022) study documents the decline in students' perception that their freedom of speech is protected. It also identifies significant differences in how Democratic- and Republican- identified students view freedom of speech and marked differences between White and Black students.

24 Daniels (2021b), p. 244. The Better Arguments Project (https://betterarguments.org), cosponsored by the nonprofit Facing History and Ourselves, the Aspen Institute's Citizenship and American Identity Program, and Allstate, offers practical methods, training, and other resources for engaging in more productive conversations on difficult subjects. The Bipartisan Policy Center's Academic Leaders Task Force on Campus Free Expression (2021) has also offered advice for campus leaders.

25 Delbanco (2022), p. 39.

26 AAC&U provides useful explanation of all HIPs (https://tinyurl.com/crakf4de): capstone courses and projects, collaborative assignments and projects, common intellectual experiences, diversity/global learning, ePortfolios, first-year seminars and experiences, internships, learning communities, service learning/community-based learning, undergraduate research, and writing-intensive courses.

27 Kuh (2008).

28 Finley & McNair (2013), p. 2.

29 Kinzie et al. (2020).

30 National Survey of Student Engagement (2019).

31 Finley & McNair (2013), p. 33.

32 For more on this subject, see Kuh and Usher (2022) and recordings of other UERU events relevant to this report available at https:// ueru.org/recordings.

33 Finley & McNair, (2013); Kuh (2013); Brownell & Swaner (2010).

34 See the useful examples of course-based research practices in first- and second-year courses in Hensel (2018).

35 See, for example, Student Experience Project (2022), Freeman et al. (2014), and Singer et al. (2012).

36 For a visual representation of what good teaching in STEM looks like, see Horii & Springborg (2022).

37 See McMurtrie (2022a) for some reasons.

38 The POD Network (https://podnetwork .org)—the professional organization for centers for teaching and learning—catalyzes, advances, and disseminates successful strategies and programs.

39 Campbell et al. (2017).

40 In a 2009 survey of all U.S. research universities (283 institutions, 95% response rate), most (83%) doctoral institutions offered one or more structured professional development programs for graduate students, 63% at R2s and 99% at R1s; some of these programs were in CTLs while others were in other institutional locations, such as graduate schools (Palmer, 2011). BrckaLorenz et al. (2020) conducted a study based on the Graduate Student Survey of Engagement, which was sent to 2500+ graduate students at eight research universities. In follow-up communication with those surveyed, BrckaLorenz and her coauthors discovered that 20% of respondents "visited an office or center that supports graduate student instructors," but higher proportions indicated that they attended a workshop to enhance their teaching (47%) or worked 1:1 with a staff or faculty member to improve their teaching (48%). This is one-year data, making it safe to say that most graduate students have some training before they complete their degrees. Significantly, a study by Connolly et al. (2016) of over 3,000 doctoral students

at three universities documented long-term teaching outcomes associated with high participation in educational development. Most (85%) respondents engaged in some professional learning by the time of graduation, but this consisted primarily of short activities. Although even a moderate degree of involvement in teaching professional development had an impact, the greatest effect was seen for those who had high levels of participation (here, defined as 55+ hours with no impact on time to degree).

41 Linse (2017).

42 Dennin et al. (2017). See also The TEval Project (https://teval.net), which engages universities in the crucial effort to develop better models for evaluating teaching, as described in Weaver et al. (2020).

43 See the virtual series National Dialogue on Transforming STEM Teaching Evaluation in Higher Education (https://tinyurl.com /5t3cbt2r) sponsored by the National Academies of Science, Engineering, and Medicine and the Board on Science Education.

44 Cited in McMurtrie (2022b). See also Fairweather (2002).

45 The Partnership for Undergraduate Life Sciences Education (PULSE) offers useful rubrics (https://pulse-community.org/rubrics) to help departments determine the extent to which they have implemented evidence-based practices.

46 Bathgate et al. (2019) and Walter et al. (2021).

47 See Wright et al. (2018).

48 See resources emerging from the Student Experience Project (callout box above) in the SEP Practices Library (https://tinyurl .com/yx7rwnn9) and the Classroom Practices Library—The College Transition Collaborative (https://tinyurl.com/2nzdppfc).

49 Light (2001), p. 81. See also Light and Jegla (2022).

50 Kuh et al. (2006), p. 60

51 Vianden (2016). See also Felten and Lambert (2020), who document the significant impact that connection to at least one faculty or staff member can have on students' long-term well-being.

52 Lyn et al. (2022). In a case study of 26 high-achieving Black male students at five historically Black colleges and universities (HBCU)s in North Carolina, Sheppard and Bryson (2022) found that holistic student advising was integral to their success.

53 Waldo (2021).

54 For one example of how the advising community is helping to advance DEIJ work, see Wesley Chamberlain and Newkirk-Kotfila (2022).

55 White (2020, June 16).

56 Smith (2013).

57 Bryant et al. (2022).

58 Zimmerman (2020), p. 233.

59 TIAA Institute (n.d.-a).

60 Pullias Center for Higher Education (2020).

61 Pullias Center for Higher Education (2020).

62 O'Meara (2022), p. 2.

63 For more on this subject, see Kezar & Maxey (2016).

64 See National Association for College Admission Counseling (NACAC) & the National Association of Student Financial Aid Administrators (NASFAA) (2022) (https://tinyurl .com/yc3xha3r).

65 Daniels, 2021a. For the argument against legacy admissions, see also McPherson (2019). According to a study of 30 highly selective universities and colleges, legacy students were three times more likely to be admitted than non-legacy students (Hurwitz, 2011). Berkeley gave up the practice in the 1990s; MIT does not practice legacy admissions and CalTech never did.

66 As of July 29, 2022, college debt had soared to a staggering $1.75 trillion across higher education (Hanson, 2022). For an overview of the negative consequences of student loan debt on students' future prospects, see Burt (2022).

67 Analysis of U.S. Department of Education, National Center for Education Statistics,

Integrated Postsecondary Education Data System (IPEDS). Analysis performed by AAU in August 2022.

68 Cahalan et al. (2022).

69 Quoted in "SEISMIC Voices" from 2021 (https://tinyurl.com/zt9d7v7w). The SEISMIC (Sloan Equity and Inclusion in STEM Introductory Courses) Collaboration is a consortium of 10 research universities: Arizona State University, Indiana University, Michigan State University, Purdue University, University of California Davis, University of California Irvine, University of California Santa Barbara, University of Michigan, University of Minnesota, and University of Pittsburgh (https://tinyurl.com/yck7j5dp).

70 The National Task Force on the Transfer and Award of Credit (2021), pp. 1,4.

71 The National Task Force on the Transfer and Award of Credit (2021), p. 36. "The gap between these groups in terms of the six-year baccalaureate completion rate is approximately 20 percentage points higher for White students compared to African-American students (45 percent versus 25 percent, respectively), and 12 percentage points higher for White students compared to Hispanic students (45 percent versus 33 percent, respectively)" (p.36).

72 The National Task Force on the Transfer and Award of Credit (2021) p. 12.

73 Davis et al. (2022).

74 The best sources on the conceptual framework guiding Arizona State University are Crow and Dabars (2015, 2020), while information on ASU's perpetually evolving suite of digital innovations and student outcomes is best accessed at https://www.asu.edu/.

75 Cited in Teich (2022).

76 McMurtrie (2021).

77 Glass (2019).

78 Melidona et al. (2021).

79 Colarossi (2022). Recent polls of U.S. college students found that 41% report having been depressed and 34% anxious; 23% report having inflicted non-suicidal self-injury in the past year, and 13% report having experienced suicidal ideation in the past year. Suicide is the second leading cause of death in 10 to 34-year-olds; 25% of young adults have contemplated suicide since the beginning of the pandemic. 45% of students agreed with the statement, "most people would think less of people who have received mental health treatment" (Eisenberg et al., 2021 and research reported by Bernadette Melnyk, VP for Health Promotion and Chief Wellness Officer, The Ohio State University, in a Boyer 2030 Commission information gathering session.) See also the Harvard Youth Poll (https://tinyurl.com/bdd375wv).

80 National Alliance on Mental Illness, p. 8.

81 Glass (2019).

82 Leshner & Scherer (2021), p. 5. Also see Murthy (2021).

83 Villalba (2020, 2021). See also the Student Experience in the Research University (SERU) study that found "among undergraduate students, major depressive disorder is more prevalent among low-income or poor and working-class students; Black or African American, Latinx, and Asian students; women, transgender, and non-binary students; gay or lesbian, bisexual, queer, questioning, asexual, and pansexual students" (Chirikov et al., 2020, p. 3).

84 Knight & Saker (2016).

85 This bipartisan bill has been endorsed by many higher education associations, including APLU and AAU (https://tinyurl.com/bdz3xfey).

86 Cited in McMurtrie (2022b).

87 University-wide academic leaders in undergraduate education enjoy many titles, including most commonly vice and associate provost and/or dean of undergraduate education. UERU refers to *all* such leaders when it uses the abbreviation UVP, which refers more narrowly to Undergraduate Vice Provost/President.

88 Boyer Commission (1998), p. 10.

89 The Colorado State University Department of Mathematics, for example, sent a team of five, including the department head, to a

Student Experience Project (SEP) meeting at the University of North Carolina at Charlotte (UNCC) in 2020, where they attended a lecture by Dr. Ibram X. Kendi (https://tinyurl.com/29hsw8xz) and collaborated with math faculty from UNCC and other SEP partner universities; the result was fundamental reform in how CSU's Department of Mathematics conceives of, and communicates with, students about pre-calculus mathematics (Jeracki, 2020). Investment by the Offices of Provost and Dean also facilitated refurbished physical tutoring and study spaces (Case, 2020). The key to these advances was department-wide faculty involvement, which directly benefited thousands of students and dovetailed with faculty research agendas, such as those of Dr. Steve Benoit (https://tinyurl.com/5b5bjdpc) and Dr. Jess Ellis Hagman (https://tinyurl.com/4r3zt9ur).

90 Daniels (2021b), p. 242.

91 Weerts et al. (2010) examined the pathway to civic engagement of college alumni and found that among college experiences campus climate, satisfaction, and learning were as significant factors in civic behavior post-college as civic engagement in college itself. Learning is a critical piece of developing civically engaged students.

92 Asai (2020), p. 754.

93 Zook & Teagle Foundation Staff (2021), pp. 3, 22.

94 Murphy & Taylor (2012).

95 Student Experience Project (2022), p. 11. See also Boucher et al. (2021).

96 Association of American Universities (2017).

97 According to Georgia State University, "Over the past decade, the university has increased our graduation rate by 23 points. We're graduating 2,800 more students a year than just five years ago and we've reduced the time to degree by half a semester, saving students $18 million a year. We've eliminated achievement gaps based on race, ethnicity or income" (https://success.gsu.edu). For more details, see Renick (2017).

98 See also Fritzsche et al. (2022).

99 Email to Elizabeth Loizeaux, July 26, 2022. "VITAL" has been championed by Lillian Nave at Appalachian State University (https://tinyurl.com/wbwher27) and adopted by the Mathematical Association of America (https://tinyurl.com/4yhwfnxx).

100 See also O'Meara (2022).

101 Harper and Kezar (n.d.-a)

102 Harper and Kezar (n.d.-b). See also Kvistad (n.d.).

103 Boyer (1990).

104 TIAA Institute (n.d.-b).

105 Howard Hughes Medical Institute (2020).

106 Nietzel (2021).

107 For a discussion of the completion problem and successful efforts to address it, see McMurtrie (2022c).

108 EDUCAUSE (2022).

References

Academic Leaders Task Force on Campus Free Expression. (2021). *Campus free expression: A new roadmap*. Bipartisan Policy Center. https://tinyurl.com/2u7zvhmt.

Advising Success Network (ASN). (2021, October 1). *Success factors for advising technology implementation: Insights from practitioners and providers to support reflection, action, and improvement.* EDUCAUSE Publications. https://tinyurl.com/ajjfbbj4.

Asai, David J. (2020). Race matters. *Cell, 181*(4), 754–757. https://doi.org/10.1016/j.cell.2020.03.044

The Association for Undergraduate Education at Research Universities. (2021, April 16). *Town hall on supporting staff and faculty mental health and well-being with Dr. Nance Roy, The Jed Foundation, and Dr. José Villalba, Wake Forest University.* https://tinyurl.com/yw2xdvru.

Association of American Colleges and Universities. (2020). *What liberal education looks like: What it is, who it's for, and where it happens.* https://tinyurl.com/ycx8c6bv.

Association of American Universities. (2017). *Progress toward achieving systemic change: A five-year status report on the AAU Undergraduate STEM Education Initiative.* https://tinyurl.com/2czzwj4x.

Bathgate, M. E., Aragón, O. R., Cavanagh, A. J., Waterhouse, J. K., Frederick, J., & Graham, M. J. (2019). Perceived supports and evidence-based teaching in college STEM. *International journal of STEM education, 6*(1), 1-14. https://doi.org/10.1186/s40594-019-0166-3.

Boucher, K., Murphy, M. C., Bartell, D., Smail, J., Logel, C., & Danek, J. (2021). Centering the student experience: What faculty and institutions can do to advance equity. *Change: The Magazine of Higher Learning, 52,* 42-50.

Boyer Commission on Educating Undergraduates in the Research University. (1998). *Reinventing undergraduate education: A blueprint for America's research universities.* Stony Brook University: Office of the President. https://tinyurl.com/23nehr2u.

Boyer Commission on Educating Undergraduates in the Research University. (2001). *Reinventing undergraduate education: Three years after the Boyer Report.* Stony Brook University: Office of the President. https://tinyurl.com/38debhmp.

Boyer, E. L. (1990). *Scholarship reconsidered: Priorities of the professoriate.* The Carnegie Foundation for the Advancement of Teaching. https://tinyurl.com/3sbs8r7a.

BrckaLorenz, A., Wang, R. & Nelson Laird, T. F. (2020). Graduate student instructors, the courses they teach, and the support they value. *New Directions for Teaching and Learning, 2020*(163), 25–34. https://doi.org/10.1002/tl.20407.

Brownell, J. E. & Swaner, L. E. (2010). *Five high-impact practices: Research on learning outcomes, completion, and quality.* American Association of Colleges and Universities. https://tinyurl.com/ys62yyp6.

Bryant, G., Shaw, C., & Bharadwaj, R. (2022). *Driving towards a degree: Closing outcome gaps through student supports.* Tyton Partners. https://tinyurl.com/4ydbabts.

Burt, C. (2022, February 9). Is your college truly meeting the financial needs of low-income students? University Business. https://tinyurl.com/2hrj73tu.

Cahalan, M. W., Addison, M., Brunt, N., Patel, P. R., Vaughan III, T., Genao, A., & Perna, L. W. (2022). *Indicators of higher education equity in the United States: 2022 historical trend report.* The Pell Institute for the Study of Opportunity in Higher Education, Council for Opportunity in Education (COE), and Alliance for Higher Education and Democracy of the University of Pennsylvania (PennAHEAD). https://tinyurl.com/2h3nznbd.

Campbell, C. M., Cabrera, A. F., Ostrow Michel, J., & Patel, S. (2017). From comprehensive to singular: A latent class analysis of college teaching practices. *Research in Higher Education, 58*(6), 581–604. https://doi.org/10.1007/s11162-016-9440-0.

Case, L. S. (2020, September). Re-envisioned: PACe becomes the Precalculus Center. *Colorado State University Source.* https://tinyurl.com/red9n2db.

Center for First-Generation Student Success. (n.d.). About the Center. Retrieved September 17, 2022, from https://tinyurl.com/bdefhrzh.

Chirikov, I., Soria, K. M., Horgos, B., & Jones-White, D. (2020). *Undergraduate and graduate students' mental health during the COVID-19 pandemic.* SERU Consortium, University of California, Berkeley and University of Minnesota. https://tinyurl.com/29jz877b.

Colarossi, J. (2022, April 28). Mental health of college students is getting worse. Boston University School of Public Health. https://tinyurl.com/45wz7267.

Commission on the Humanities and Social Sciences. (2013). *The heart of the matter: The humanities and social sciences for a vibrant, competitive, and secure nation.* American Academy of Arts and Sciences. https://tinyurl.com/y8tn26b5.

Connolly, M. R., Savoy, J. N., Lee, Y.-G., & Hill, L. B. (2016). *Building a better future STEM faculty: How teaching development programs can improve undergraduate education.* Wisconsin Center for Education Research. https://www.cirtl.net/resources/901.

Crow, M., & Dabars, W. (2015, September 28). Go big. Go really big. *Politico.* https://tinyurl.com/ms4ap9h2.

Crow, M., & Dabars, W. (2020). *The fifth wave: The evolution of American higher education.* Johns Hopkins University Press. https://www.doi.org/10.1353/book.73164.

Daniels, R. J. (2021a, October 7). Abolish legacy admissions now: Hereditary advantage has no place in higher ed. *The Chronicle Review.* https://tinyurl.com/5t3duyps.

Daniels, R. J. (with Shreve, G., & Spector, P.). (2021b). *What universities owe democracy.* Johns Hopkins University Press. https://doi.org/10.1353/book.97330.

Davidson, C. N. (2017). *The new education: How to revolutionize the university to prepare students for a world in flux.* Basic Books.

Davis, L., Pocai, J., Taylor, J. L., Kauppila, S. A., & Rubin, P. (2022). *Lighting the path to remove systemic barriers in higher education and award earned postsecondary credentials through IHEP's Degrees When Due initiative.* Institute for Higher Education Policy. https://tinyurl.com/yptsdrvf.

Delbanco, A. (2012). *College: What it was, is, and should be.* Princeton University Press.

Delbanco, A. (2022, February 7). The university crisis: Does the pandemic mark a breaking point? *The Nation,* (February 21/28, 2022). https://tinyurl.com/3c7s9re7.

Dennin, M., Schultz, Z. D., Feig, A., Finkelstein, N., Follmer Greenhoot, A., Hildreth, M., Leibovich, A. K., Martin, J. D., Moldwin, M. B., O'Dowd, D. K., Posey, L. A., Smith, T. L., & Miller, E. R. (2017). Aligning practice to policies: Changing the culture to recognize and reward teaching at research universities. *CBE—Life Sciences Education, 16*(4). https://doi.org/10.1187/cbe.17-02-0032.

Eisenberg, D., Lipson, S. K., & Heinze, J. (2021). *The healthy minds study: 2021 winter/spring data report.* The Healthy Minds Network. https://tinyurl.com/39bhu3sm.

Fairweather, J. S. (2002). The ultimate faculty evaluation: Promotion and tenure decisions. *New Directions for Institutional Research, 2020*(114), 97–108. https://doi.org/10.1002/ir.50.

Felten, P. & Lambert, L. M. (2020). *Relationship-rich education: How human connections drive success in college.* Johns Hopkins University Press. http://doi.org/10.1353/book.78561.

Finley, A. (2021). *How college contributes to workforce success: Employer views on what matters most.* American Association of Colleges and Universities. https://tinyurl.com/2rzx7t38.

Finley, A. & McNair, T. B. (2013). *Assessing underserved students' engagement in high-impact practices.* American Association of Colleges and Universities. https://tinyurl.com/yetpr78f.

Fischman, W. & Gardner, H. (2022a). *The real world of college: What higher education is and what it can be.* MIT Press. https://doi.org/10.7551/mitpress/13652.001.0001.

Fischman, W. & Gardner, H. (2022b, May 25). Students are missing the point of college. *The Chronicle Review*. https://tinyurl.com/mrn6ara7.

Fitzpatrick, K. (2019). *Generous thinking: A radical approach to saving the university*. Johns Hopkins University Press.

Freeman, S., Eddy, S. L., McDonough, M., Smith, M. K., Okoroafor, N., Jordt, H., & Wenderoth, M. P. (2014). Active learning increases student performance in science, engineering, and mathematics. *Proceedings of the National Academy of Sciences, 111*(23), 8410–8415. https://doi .org/10.1073/pnas.1319030111.

Fritzsche, S., Hart-Davidson, W., & Long, C. P. (2022). Charting pathways of intellectual leadership: An initiative for transformative personal and institutional change. *Change: The Magazine of Higher Learning, 54*(3), 19–27. https://doi.org/10.1080/00091383.2022.2054175.

Gavazzi, S. M. & Gee, E. G. (2018). *Land-grant universities for the future: Higher education for the public good*. Johns Hopkins University Press. https://doi.org/10.1353/book.62441.

Glass, G. (2019, May 29). Rethinking campus mental health. *Inside Higher Ed*. https://tinyurl .com/4r9p2ner.

Hanson, M. (2022, July 29). Student loan debt statistics. Education Data Initiative. https://tinyurl .com/2tz5vv6r.

Harper, J. & Kezar, A. (n.d.-a). *Systemic Improvement for teaching faculty and expansion of tenure for teaching at Worcester Polytechnic Institute (WPI)*. Retrieved September 17, 2022, from https://tinyurl .com/yxa83scw.

Harper, J. & Kezar, A. (n.d.-b). *Institutionalizing a culture of respect for teaching and professional faculty at the University of Denver*. Retrieved September 17, 2022, from https://tinyurl.com/t2zzx3rb.

Hart Research Associates. (2018). *Fulfilling the American dream: Liberal education and the future of work, selected findings from online surveys of business executives and hiring managers*. Association of American Colleges and Universities. https://tinyurl.com/y2ms4wah.

Hensel, N. H. (Ed.). (2018). *Course-based undergraduate research: Educational equity and high-impact practice*. Stylus Publishing.

Hora, M. T. (with Benbow, R. J. and Oleson, A. K.). (2016). *Beyond the skills gap: Preparing college students for life and work*. Harvard Education Press.

Horii, C. V. & Springborg, M. (2022). *What teaching looks like: Higher education through photographs*. Elon University Center for Engaged Learning. https://doi.org/10.36284/celelon.oa4.

Howard Hughes Medical Institute. (2020). *Driving Change institutional self-study guide*. https://tinyurl .com/ycyws34t.

The Humanities Indicators Project. (2021). *State of the humanities 2021: Workforce & beyond*. American Academy of Arts and Sciences. https://tinyurl.com/2wks27a2.

Hurwitz, M. (2011). The impact of legacy status on undergraduate admissions at elite colleges and universities. *Economics of Education Review, 30*(3), 480–492, https://doi.org/10.1016/j. econedurev.2010.12.002.

Jaschik, S. & Lederman, D. (2022, May 11). Provosts stand firm in academic survey. *Inside Higher Ed*. https://tinyurl.com/56hy95yf.

Jeracki, K. (2020, February). Changing mindsets for student success through the Student Experience Project. *Colorado State University Source*. https://tinyurl.com/47h6xd.

Kezar, A. & Maxey, D. (2016). Resonant themes for a professoriate reconsidered: Consensus points to organize efforts toward change. In A. Kezar & D. Maxey (Eds.), *Envisioning the faculty for the 21st century: Moving to a mission-oriented and learner-centered model* (pp. 204–215). Rutgers University Press.

Kinzie, J., McCormick, A. C., Gonyea, R., Dugan, B., & Silberstein, S. (2020). *Assessing quality and equity in high-impact practices: Comprehensive report*. Indiana University Center for Postsecondary Research. https://tinyurl.com/bddv9st6.

Knight, C., & Saker, A. (2016, May 22). For Ono, the time to speak about mental health is now. *Cincinnati Enquirer*. https://tinyurl.com/yrp7cbhs.

Knight Foundation-Ipsos. (2022, January). *College student views on free expression and campus speech 2022: A look at key trends in student speech views since 2016*. https://tinyurl.com/bdds5zws.

Kuh, G. D. (2008). *High-impact educational practices: What they are, who has access to them, and why they matter*. American Association of Colleges and Universities. https://tinyurl.com/2p9dezaz.

Kuh, G. D. (2013). *Ensuring quality and taking high-impact practices to scale*. American Association of Colleges and Universities. https://tinyurl.com/5n88tkk8.

Kuh, G. D., Kinzie, J., Buckley, J. A., Bridges, B. K., & Hayek, J. C. (2006). *What matters to student success: A review of the literature*. National Postsecondary Education Cooperative. https://tinyurl.com/2stzj5pd.

Kuh, G. D. & Usher, B. (2022, August 1). *High-impact practices today: A focus on equity* [Webinar]. Association for Undergraduate Education at Research Universities Town Hall, Online. https://tinyurl.com/dk7sb5rh.

Kvistad, G. (n.d.). What key considerations should guide redesigning the academic workforce? TIAA Institute. Retrieved September 17, 2022, from https://tinyurl.com/jm5env4n.

Leshner, A. I., & Scherer, L. A. (2021). Mental health, substance use, and wellbeing in higher education: Supporting the whole student. *The National Academies Press*. https://doi.org/10.17226/26015.

Light, R. J. (2001). *Making the most of college: Students speak their minds*. Harvard University Press.

Light, R. J. & Jegla, A. (2022). *Becoming great universities: Small steps for sustained excellence*. Princeton University Press.

Linse, A. R. (2017). Interpreting and using student ratings data: Guidance for faculty serving as administrators and on evaluation committees. *Studies in Educational Evaluation, 54*, 94–106. https://doi.org/10.1016/j.stueduc.2016.12.004.

Lyn, J. S., Hilliard, K. A., & Seabold, J. A. (Eds.). (2022). *Advising at HBCUs: A resource collection advancing educational equity and student success*. University of South Carolina, National Resource Center for The First-Year Experience and Students in Transition. https://tinyurl.com/3zusw46u.

Montás, R. (2021). *Rescuing Socrates: How the great books saved my life and why they matter for a new generation*. Princeton University Press.

Montás, R. (2022, January 19). *Liberal education: For what and for whom?* [The Carol Geary Schneider Lecture on Liberal Education and Inclusive Excellence]. AAC&U 2022 Annual Meeting, Washington, DC, United States.

McMurtrie, B. (2021, July 28). Is your degree program too complicated? Poor design and needless bloat are derailing students. *The Chronicle of Higher Education*. https://tinyurl.com/5fcctst9.

McMurtrie, B. (2022a, January 3). Why the science of teaching is often ignored. *The Chronicle of Higher Education*. https://tinyurl.com/ykd6nhy6.

McMurtrie, B. (2022b, February 10). What stands in the way of better teaching? College leaders. *The Chronicle of Higher Education Teaching Newsletter*. https://tinyurl.com/3u5ud3an.

McMurtrie, B. (2022c, June 17). The student-success challenge: Engineering a better college experience requires more than tinkering around the edges. *The Chronicle of Higher Education*. https://tinyurl.com/47kwspyj.

McPherson, P. (2019, March 21). Creating a legacy of fairness in admissions. *Inside Higher Ed*. https://tinyurl.com/5daszcxd.

Melidona, D., Taylor, M., & McNamee, T. C. (2021, October 25). *2021 fall term Pulse Point survey of college and university presidents*. American Council on Education. https://tinyurl.com/4m7shk22.

The Morrill Act of 1862, 7 U.S.C. § 304 *et seq.* (1862). https://tinyurl.com/56zb85bs.

Murphy, M. C., & Taylor, V. J. (2012). The role of situational cues in signaling and maintaining stereotype threat. In M. Inzlicht & T. Schmader (Eds.), *Stereotype threat: Theory, process, and application* (pp. 17–33). Oxford University Press.

Murthy, V. H. (2021). *Protecting youth mental health: The U.S. surgeon general's advisory*. Office of the Surgeon General, US Department of Health and Human Services. https://tinyurl.com/bdru69cc.

National Alliance for Mental Illness. (2012). *College students speak: A survey report on mental health*. https://tinyurl.com/4ykdfvwh.

National Association for College Admission Counseling & the National Association of Student Financial Aid Administrators. (2022). *Toward a more equitable future for postsecondary access*. https://tinyurl.com/yc3xha3r.

National Survey of Student Engagement. (2019). *Engagement insights: Survey findings on the quality of undergraduate education*. Indiana University Center for Postsecondary Research. https://tinyurl.com/6vttr7kn.

The National Task Force on the Transfer and Award of Credit. (2021). *Reimagining transfer for student success*. American Council on Education. https://tinyurl.com/2p8n7uyw.

Nietzel, M. T. (2021, November 19). University of California reaches final decision: No more standardized admission testing. *Forbes*. https://tinyurl.com/2pwt6fvx.

O'Meara, K. (2022). *Enabling possibility: Reform of faculty appointments and evaluation*. TIAA Institute. https://tinyurl.com/3wswyzzt.

Palmer, M. S. (2011). Graduate student professional development: A decade after calls for national reform. In L. L. B. Border (Ed.), *Mapping the range of graduate student professional development*, (pp. 1–17). New Forums Press.

Pasquerella, L. (2022). *What we value: Public health, social justice, and educating for democracy*. University of Virginia Press.

Pullias Center for Higher Education. (2020, May). *Selected research on connections between non-tenure-track faculty and student learning*. University of Southern California. https://tinyurl.com/mry8h9ec.

Renick, T. M. (2017, May 4). *Leveraging technology and data to eliminate postsecondary achievement gaps* [PowerPoint Slides]. Ed Tech Efficacy Research Symposium, Washington, DC. https://tinyurl.com/229d52fb.

Sheppard, W. & Bryson, B. S. (2022). HBCUs in North Carolina: Holistic student support toward Black male students. In J. S. Lyn, K. A. Hilliard, & J. A. Seabold (Eds.), *Advising at HBCUs: A resource collection advancing educational equity and student success*. University of South Carolina, National Resource Center for The First-Year Experience and Students in Transition. https://tinyurl.com/3zusw46u.

Singer, S. R., Nielsen, N. R., & Schweingruber, H. A. (Eds.). (2012). *Discipline-based education research: Understanding and improving learning in undergraduate science and engineering*. National Academies Press. https://doi.org/10.17226/13362.

Smith, J. S. (2013). Chapter 9. In A. Carlstrom & M. A. Miller (Eds.), *NACADA 2011 National Survey of Academic Advising* (Monograph No. 25). National Academic Advising Association.

Student Experience Project. (2022). *Increasing equity in college student experience: Findings from a national collaborative*. https://tinyurl.com/4jut93zv.

Teich, A. G. (2022, April 7). *ASU president Michael Crow addresses future of higher education*. Fierce Education. https://tinyurl.com/haz6y3d6.

Thorp, H., & Goldstein, B. (2018). *Our higher calling: Rebuilding the partnership between America and its colleges and universities*. University of North Carolina Press.

TIAA Institute. (n.d.-a). *Higher education workforce trends: Evolving faculty patterns*. Retrieved September 17, 2022, from https://tinyurl.com/y3xkuvjb.

TIAA Institute. (n.d.-b). *Higher education workforce trends: Publications*. Retrieved September 17, 2022, from https://tinyurl.com/5n8v64ya.

Vianden, J. (2016). Ties that bind: Academic advisors as agents of student relationship management. *NACADA Journal, 36*(1), 19–29. https://doi.org/10.12930/NACADA-15-026a.

Villalba, J. (2020, November 17). 3 campus groups that especially need support. *Insider Higher Ed.* https://tinyurl.com/mr2sfu2n.

Villalba, J. (2021, January 20). The unbearable labor of understanding. *Inside Higher Ed.* https://tinyurl.com/7mp8rs2.

Waldo, E. (2021, June 11). A Goodbye Q&A with Eric Waldo. *Forbes.* https://tinyurl.com/48mb599h.

Walter, E. M., Beach, A. L., Henderson, C., Williams, C. T., & Ceballos-Madrigal, I. (2021). Understanding conditions for teaching innovation in postsecondary education: Development and validation of the Survey of Climate for Instructional Improvement (SCII). *International Journal of Technology in Education (IJTE), 4*(2), 166–199. https://doi.org/10.46328/ijte.46.

Weaver, G. C., Austin, A. E., Follmer Greenhoot, A., & Finkelstein, N. D. (2020). Establishing a better approach for evaluating teaching: The TEval Project. *The Magazine of Higher Learning, 52*(3), 25–31. https://doi.org/10.1080/00091383.2020.1745575.

Weerts, D. J., Cabrera, A. F. & Sanford, T. (2010). Beyond giving: Political advocacy and volunteer behaviors of public university alumni. *Research in Higher Education, 51*(4), 346–365. https://doi.org/10.1007/s11162-009-9158-3.

Wellbeing Collaborative at Wake Forest University. (n.d.). *Wellbeing dimensions and more.* Retrieved September 17, 2022, from https://tinyurl.com/yc868z7z.

Wesley Chamberlain, A., & Newkirk-Kotfila, E. (2022). *(Mis)Understanding students: Approaches to affirming student identities.* National Association of Student Personnel Administrators (NASPA). https://tinyurl.com/mw9jv922.

White, E. R. (2020, June 16). Academic advising in a pandemic and beyond. *Inside Higher Ed.* https://tinyurl.com/mrxda8yt.

Wright, M. (2023). *Centers for teaching and learning: The new landscape in higher education.* Johns Hopkins University Press.

Wright, M., Horii, C. V., Felten, P., Sorcinelli, M. D., & Kaplan, M. (2018). *Faculty development improves teaching and learning* [White paper]. POD Network. https://tinyurl.com/bdhxax9k.

Zimmerman, J. (2020). *The amateur hour: A history of college teaching in America.* Johns Hopkins University Press. https://doi.org/10.1353/book.77834.

Zook, M., & Teagle Foundation Staff. (2021). *Revitalizing the role of the humanities in general education.* The Teagle Foundation; National Endowment for the Humanities. https://tinyurl.com/3ctnxsnr.

Appendix A. Association for Undergraduate Education at Research Universities (UERU) Boyer 2030 Commission UERU Member Questionnaire: July 2021

Summary

The July 2021 qualitative survey of the member institutions of the Association for Undergraduate Education at Research Universities (UERU) was intended to give the Boyer 2030 Commission the benefit of the experience and perspective of the campus leaders (the undergraduate vice provosts/presidents) responsible for undergraduate education at their institutions. These leaders are the core of UERU. They know intimately what's happening on the ground. They will be responsible for implementing the recommendations of Boyer 2030. The analytically sharp, sometimes moving, responses offer a window onto their most pressing concerns, their successes and challenges, their aspirations, and their dedication to the 2.5 million students UERU members serve every year. The responses provide a window into the current state of undergraduate education at research universities.

Nearly 60 percent of UERU members representing public and private universities participated in the survey.

Following is a brief synthesis of important themes, followed by a summary and some representative responses to selected questions.

Overview of Results

- **Equity**, in its many manifestations and ramifications, must be central to the reform agenda going forward (and in ways that were perhaps not as evident in 1998). Access to the university clearly matters, but so, too, does access (real access) to educational and career-exploration opportunities.

- **Economics** cannot be elided, including the value proposition of higher education for students and how we explain it as well as funding disparities within research universities.

- **Excellence** raises many questions: How should we define it? What is distinctive about research universities' pursuit of it? Who is responsible for ensuring it? How do we fairly assess it?

Other important themes include the following:

- *Academic advising* is on many minds, including how to offer consistent, holistic guidance focused on exploration, growth, and advice on educational and career opportunities and pathways.

- *General education* remains an endemic problem/challenge; it needs strengthening and updating for the 21st century ("reimagining the liberal arts"), it needs to be broad ("enlightening"), and it needs to resist overemphasis on workforce readiness. "Most of us, including my own institution, are running with distribution models of general education that reach back to the mid-20th century (requirement tweaks and various re-naming/re-labeling initiatives notwithstanding). It's time for a reconsideration," noted one respondent.

- *Inclusive pedagogy* is also on many minds, with considerable frustration at our failure to train graduate students in even basic, effective, research-grounded pedagogy—and to require it of our faculty. The cycle repeats. "Quality of instruction is just as problematic now as it was during the Boyer Report years," one respondent observed. There is a lack of alignment between institutional claims about excellent undergraduate education taught by leading researchers and the faculty reward system, especially for tenured/tenure track faculty. "There aren't enough awards/compensation for great faculty, and there is no consequence for inadequate or incompetent teaching," replied one participant. And faculty members—our institutions—aren't used to thinking about the best interests of students—though the pandemic offered hope that they can.

- *Diversity* of institutional character, mission, region, and, frankly, political circumstance, emerged as vexing for achieving any would-be overarching set of standards and recommendations.

In the responses, one also senses an acute mixture of post-pandemic anticipation and pent-up frustration with the pace and efficacy of previous reform efforts. Observed one participant, "It is vital that we don't lose these lessons [of the pandemic], so it's now incumbent on us all to avoid a return to normal, and instead reimagine a future in which residential education is much better than it was before the pandemic." Strong leadership and support at the top lie behind most successful, enduring improvements in undergraduate education.

It's as though UERU members are asking, Can the Boyer 2030 Commission distill complexity to provide clarity of vision and method, guide innovation on behalf of shared albeit broad goals, and encourage truly bold leadership? In keeping with our era's renewed and heightened awareness of institutional and cultural barriers, can research universities discern and then effect deep-seated reform at the level of policy as well as practice?

Summary of Selected Boyer 2030 Commission UERU Questionnaire Responses

Q1. What do you see as the single most important improvement that has been made in undergraduate education on your campus in recent years?

Many responses described a growth in the importance placed on student success. This took the form of new emphasis on academic advising; the deployment of actionable analytics to track and improve retention and graduation rates; and a focus on diversity, equity, and inclusion. Many campuses implemented new core curricula that gave experiential and active learning a new and central role in undergraduate education.

- **Verbatim 1:** "A growth in student-centered models in and out of the classroom. A move away from 'sink or swim' type frameworks and mentalities from faculty. A growth of student support mechanisms. A shift of diversity, equity and inclusion into the mainstream and into the core of our academic mission."

- **Verbatim 2:** "The implementation of a mandatory experiential learning requirement for graduation."

- **Verbatim 3:** "A general shift toward reducing barriers and supporting students in overcoming barriers."

Q1A. Who or what factors had the biggest influence on making that improvement come about?

Respondents credited student activism and new roles for student voices as drivers of improvements in undergraduate education. Others highlighted the impact made by university leadership, faculty, and offices of institutional research. Almost every response highlighted the collaborative efforts that led to positive change. In some cases, improvements came about because of the COVID-19 pandemic.

- **Verbatim 1:** "Fueled by lots of research, conversation, and professional development. No single one person, but more of a collective that spans all levels."
- **Verbatim 2:** "The President's commitment to making the requirement be implemented."
- **Verbatim 3:** "Mandate from President."
- **Verbatim 4:** "Students and prospective students verbalized that they were looking for engagement in the classroom."

Q2. If you could wave a wand and magically change one thing in undergraduate education at your university, what would it be?

Eliminating barriers for student success and giving students more of a safety net, such as smaller classes, more support for students of color and first year students, and removing weed-out courses were core responses for "waving a magic wand." Opportunity for undergraduates to participate in research or research-like experiences, including mentored research experiences, was also emphasized. Several comments referenced making education more personalized and relevant for students and having more centralized and holistic student support. A few respondents focused on changing faculty tenure and promotion policies to recognize teaching and service (e.g., mentoring) in the tenure and merit review process.

- **Verbatim 1:** "Changes to the faculty merit, promotion, and tenure policies and apparatuses to more clearly and incisively reward teaching and mentoring at the undergraduate level."
- **Verbatim 2:** "Eliminate the double-whammy punishments for students struggling academically: eliminate early course drop deadlines, eliminate 'workload' preparatory/remedial courses that are required but don't count toward degree or graduation, stop bundling the GPA penalty and the degree-progress penalty when students fail a class, etc. It almost seems like when a student starts to struggle, we are trying to kick them out as quickly as possible. The system doesn't really allow for students to recover from the steep learning curve that some of them encounter—classes, homesickness, culture shock, adulting, etc. We should give them more of a safety net, even a small one."
- **Verbatim 3:** "Student services would be seamlessly integrated across a single platform allowing students to access support and resources for academic choices, financial planning, and personal milestones. For example, this tool would allow students to see instantly how changes in academic choices would affect their personal finances, what skills they would gain from each offering, and how those skills could be marketed to particular careers. Individualized development plans could be tied to data-driven suggestions for students to act on."

Q3. Are there any new practices that your campus implemented in response to the pandemic that you think should be preserved as universities move back to more "normal" operations?

Many responses discussed the transition to remote services, such as online courses and online advising, and the power of technology in education. Others mentioned enhanced mental health services and advising faculty about good student mental health practices. Rethinking withdrawal and pass/fail policies was also mentioned.

- **Verbatim 1:** "Online advising and tutoring were very helpful. Offering some STEM courses online to improve flexibility and assist working students has been helpful and should continue. Zoom has made us much more efficient in our time by shortening physical travel and benefiting employees who can work from home."

- **Verbatim 2:** "Promote good student mental health practices with faculty—acknowledge that faculty can be the first line of defense (or the only person who notices) when a student is struggling, and equip them with the knowledge, resources, and process to listen, to accommodate, to refer, and to call an emergency when they see one. A few faculty felt like this 'new role' was an imposition. Most were extremely grateful."

- **Verbatim 3:** "We have embraced synchronous, distance education and are launching a number of degrees in that format in fall 2021. This new modality is envisioned as a crucial tool to expand access to higher education. In particular, it is valuable for those who have some university but have not completed because life got in the way but do not find success in asynchronous coursework. Similarly, it offers a path to graduate and professional education for a broader array of individuals with significant non-academic commitments."

Q4. List the three most important issues you think the commission should address.

Issues most commonly listed were increasing accessibility; addressing diversity and equity; promoting experiential, engaged, and active learning; and promoting faculty engagement in student success. Other issues brought up multiple times were the technology gap, grading practices, exploitation of non-tenured adjunct faculty, curriculum reform, student debt, accreditation, standardized testing, student well-being, and the perceived value of higher education by the public.

- **Verbatim 1:** "1. Equity. 2. Equity. 3. Equity. It probably seems like I'm being facetious. I'm not. Higher education should be an engine of social mobility. The demographics of the college-going population in this country are changing dramatically (and have already changed, in my state)—non-white, low-income, and first-generation. But if we are only really serving the students we've always been good at serving, and just giving some kind of false bootstrapping 'opportunity' to everyone else, we may as well just endorse feudalism already."

- **Verbatim 2:** "1. Schools with low retention/graduation rates. 2. Affordability and access. 3. Encouraging adoption of experiential learning, including course credit."

Q5. What do you see as the most innovative approaches your campus has taken in recent years to assure fair and equitable access to your university for prospective undergraduate students?

Recent admissions policy changes, such as making admissions test-optional or ending legacy admissions, were a major theme. Also mentioned were efforts to address affordability through new programs and scholarships as well as reforms to the core curriculum for first-year students. Some responses were deeply pessimistic about the approaches undertaken (or not) on their campuses.

- **Verbatim 1:** "None. We're 77% male and overwhelmingly white. We aren't innovative about access and we have massive achievement gaps for Pell and URM [underrepresented minority] students."

- **Verbatim 2:** "We changed our admissions targets, with a goal of having 20% of our students be Pell-eligible (from just 6% eight years ago)."

- **Verbatim 3:** "The pandemic has caused us to look at far fewer applicants with standardized test scores; that may not be innovative (it's happening everywhere) but it has certainly helped us counteract the biases inherent in those tests and their use. One innovative approach we have taken is focusing on students who live in an area closely adjacent to our campus . . . . We have a new program that supports public school students who live in 8 zip codes close to campus with full scholarships and a summer bridge program to help them adjust to life as a . . . student [at our institution]."

Q6. What do you see as effective strategies to support faculty members in using inclusive, effective, and innovative pedagogical practices on your campus?

Campus teaching centers that provide training and other professional development opportunities for faculty were an often-cited strategy. Incentivizing faculty to participate in training programs through time releases, department-based competitions, fellowships, or summer salaries was also mentioned. In some instances, responses discussed using data, such as retention rates and graduation rates, disaggregated by race, ethnicity, socioeconomic status, and gender to understand the success of students in different contexts.

- **Verbatim 1:** "Having the right incentives coupled with just-in-time support. Most faculty value equity and desire to be inclusive in their classrooms. However, most faculty struggle to spend the time to make the changes necessary (and many are often unaware of the many challenges faced by their students). Providing the right information and support at the right moment will help. Providing some incentives (time, rather than money) would help many faculty take the necessary steps."

- **Verbatim 2:** "Creating cohort programs so faculty can engage in this work together and providing professional development funds and/or release time to compensate faculty for putting time into these cohorts, wherein they actually redesign their courses, not just add tweaks around the edges. But this level of time investment is unlikely, since it takes away from research (which is how faculty are rewarded), unless it is compensated in some way."

- **Verbatim 3:** "Hold departments and colleges accountable for their performance, measured in terms of retention rates and graduation rates, disaggregated by race, ethnicity, socio-economic status, and gender."

Q10. What do you see as the most influential forms of evidence to measure and document student success?

Analysis of student data such as retention rates, graduation rates, student debt default rates, and numbers of students dropping/failing from classes were core here. These data should be examined and broken out by race, ethnicity, income, first-generation status, and other identities. Use of surveys, such as the National Survey of Student Engagement, and climate assessments was also suggested. In some instances, responses focused on the importance of student testimonials and defining what student "success" means.

- **Verbatim 1:** "Student videos and testimonials. They have an incredible impact on families, prospective students, and trustees."

- **Verbatim 2:** "Analysis of student data and patterns. We need to see how students from different groups (declared major at entrance, final major, Pell status, race/ethnicity, gender, first-gen, native/transfer, geographic origin) move through our systems so that we can address issues that prevent completion, and identify successful activities that can be replicated. We also need to expand the definition of success—community college completion may be success in some fields, while transfer from one four-year to another could be another success if that meets the students' goals. But, unfortunately, I don't know how to measure that! At the same time, we need to evaluate student learning around major objectives of universities and degree programs, to make sure that we aren't prioritizing degree production over knowledge and skills gained—creating true systems of inclusive excellence."

- **Verbatim 3:** "There are a variety of measures, and it depends on how you define success (retention, graduation, post-bac employment, social mobility, etc.). But whatever you do, you have to look at demographic equity (race, gender, income, first-gen status), or you risk masking serious underlying problems with larger metrics that render these differences invisible."

Appendix B. World Readiness: Some Questions for Campus Conversations

Q1. How well is your university providing education for world readiness?

Questions to consider:

- What *do* our students need to succeed in life, work, and democratic citizenship in the 21st century?

- What distinctive opportunities does our university offer that we could bring to bear on providing education for world readiness?

- Do all students have sufficient opportunity to wrestle with important, difficult questions for society; thoughtfully construct arguments and examine current and historical evidence for claims; and practice engaging in civil discourse with peers who have diverse backgrounds and viewpoints?

- Do all students get sufficient breadth of exposure to major issues and ways of thinking across disciplines?

- Do all students have sufficient space in their degree program for exploration across the university—essential for identifying interests, expanding understanding and sympathy for other viewpoints, exercising curiosity, and developing skills for lifelong learning? Does space for exploration need to be hardwired into university and/or major requirements?

  - If students in high-requirement majors do not have sufficient opportunity for exploration, should a maximum number of credits required for undergraduate majors (and degrees) be considered? Most universities require a minimum. What about a maximum?

- Do all students have sufficient opportunity—in multiple courses—to develop communication skills (written, oral/signed, multimedia) so important to employers and necessary for exercising complex reasoning skills and the ability to deal with uncertainty and nuance?

- How do students acquire an understanding of environmental issues and the need for a sustainable relationship between the built environment and the natural environment?

- If it does not exist in the curriculum for all students already, where might education in and reflection on democracy in a diverse society be built in as an essential cornerstone of undergraduate education? Should there be a "Democracy Requirement," as Ronald Daniels, president of Johns Hopkins University, has advocated?[90]

- How can we best develop students' abilities as critical consumers and makers of online media so that they understand the power and perils of digital culture and are themselves empowered in their use of it, not passive recipients and resigned victims of it?

- How can we best develop students' ability to understand scientific concepts and how scientific research is done?

- How can we best develop students' ability to understand and critically interpret data?

- Where do, or could, all students have the opportunity to work in diverse teams, supervised by an instructor with expertise in fostering teamwork? Employers want it; our democracy needs it.

- What role do, or could, student affairs staff play in educating for world readiness? Colleges and universities are increasingly experimenting with cocurricular transcripts to recognize and record learning outside the classroom. Is that a route to take? Where might there be opportunities for academic affairs and student affairs to work together and to develop the much-needed understanding of what's involved in the work each does in educating our students?

Q2. How well is your university communicating the purpose, content, and breadth of an education that prepares students for life, work, and engaged citizenship over a lifetime, an education for world readiness?

Questions to consider:

- Do we clearly articulate both how we educate for long-term career accomplishment and how we support students in making the college to career transition, whether that be a first job, graduate school, or another pathway to meaningful work?
  - Do we provide evidence, with data, of the interrelationship between liberal education and lifelong career success and satisfaction, as well as life satisfaction and civic engagement?[91]
- Do we communicate this message to all stakeholders and embed it in appropriate places in such routine communications as letters to parents, students, donors, legislators?

Q3. How well is your university supporting students in gaining knowledge and skills for the next step after college and making that crucial connection to a first post-college step along a career path, be that a job, graduate school, or another endeavor?

Questions to consider:

- What do our data on connections to first jobs for our graduates tell us about what's working for students, what's not, what's in place, what's not? Do we have the data necessary to answer this question? If not, how can we get it?
- How well are we doing in making the connection to a first job for our low-income and first-generation students? Are the connections we help make working as a sustainable pathway for all students, looking, perhaps, 1, 2, 5 and 10 years out?
- How well are we connecting students to such opportunities to develop a career path as internships, community-based projects, or part-time work on or off campus?
- How well are our academic advisors equipped to advise students about the importance of, and give them help in, gaining the experience necessary for a first job? This is especially important for low-income and first-generation students who may not know, for example, to seek help in obtaining a summer job or paid internship that helps them explore possible careers as well as pay for college.
- How effective are alumni networks in providing practical advice and help connecting students to first jobs? Alums may be especially critical to students majoring in

nonprofessional fields where faculty members are less able than in professional programs to facilitate connections to the array of jobs outside the academy available to their students.

- Do we, can we, continue to support our graduates beyond graduation to make the connection beyond a first job to a career path? A number of universities now offer their alums lifetime connections to their career centers and offer long-post-graduation advice for those in career transitions.

Appendix C. U.S. Research Universities

Following are the institutions classified by the Carnegie Foundation for the Advancement of Teaching and the American Council on Education as R1/2 research universities in 2021.

Denotes UERU membership at time of this report's publication.

Air Force Institute of Technology-Graduate School of Engineering & Management

American University*

Arizona State University Campus Immersion*

Arizona State University Digital Immersion

Arkansas State University

Auburn University

Augusta University

Azusa Pacific University

Ball State University

Baylor University*

Binghamton University

Boise State University

Boston College*

Boston University*

Bowling Green State University*

Brandeis University

Brigham Young University

Brown University*

California Institute of Technology

California State University, East Bay

California State University, Fresno

California State University, Fullerton

California State University, Long Beach

California State University, San Bernardino

Carnegie Mellon University*

Case Western Reserve University

The Catholic University of America

Central Michigan University

Chapman University

Claremont Graduate University

Clark Atlanta University*

Clark University

Clarkson University

Clemson University*

Cleveland State University

Colorado School of Mines

Colorado State University at Fort Collins*

Columbia University

Cornell University

Creighton University

CUNY City College

CUNY Graduate School and University Center

Dartmouth College

DePaul University

Drexel University

Duke University*

Duquesne University

East Carolina University

East Tennessee State University

Eastern Michigan University

Emory University*

Florida Agricultural and Mechanical University

Florida Atlantic University

Florida Institute of Technology

Florida International University*

Florida State University*

Fordham University

George Mason University*

George Washington University

Georgetown University

Georgia Institute of Technology*

Georgia Southern University

Georgia State University*

Harvard University

Howard University*

Idaho State University

Illinois Institute of Technology

Illinois State University

Indiana University of Pennsylvania
Indiana University Bloomington*
Indiana University Purdue University Indianapolis*
Iowa State University*
Jackson State University
James Madison University
Johns Hopkins University*
Kansas State University*
Kennesaw State University
Kent State University*
Lehigh University
Loma Linda University
Long Island University
Louisiana State University and Agricultural & Mechanical College
Louisiana Tech University
Loyola Marymount University
Loyola University Chicago
Marquette University*
Marshall University
Massachusetts Institute of Technology
Mercer University
Miami University, Oxford
Michigan State University*
Michigan Technological University
Middle Tennessee State University
Mississippi State University
Missouri University of Science and Technology*
Montana State University
Montclair State University*
Morgan State University*
New Jersey Institute of Technology
New Mexico State University*
The New School
New York University
North Carolina A & T State University
North Carolina State University*
North Dakota State University
Northeastern University
Northern Arizona University
Northern Illinois University

Northwestern University*
Nova Southeastern University
Oakland University
Ohio State University*
Ohio University
Oklahoma State University*
Old Dominion University
Oregon State University
The Pennsylvania State University*
Portland State University
Prairie View A & M University
Princeton University
Purdue University*
Rensselaer Polytechnic Institute
Rice University
Rochester Institute of Technology
Rowan University
Rutgers University–Camden
Rutgers University–New Brunswick*
Rutgers University–Newark*
Saint Louis University*
Sam Houston State University
San Diego State University
San Francisco State University
Seton Hall University
South Dakota State University
Southern Illinois University Carbondale
Southern Methodist University*
Southern University and A&M College
Stanford University
Stevens Institute of Technology
Stony Brook University*
SUNY College of Environmental Science and Forestry
Syracuse University*
Tarleton State University
Teachers College at Columbia University
Temple University*
Tennessee State University
Tennessee Technological University
Texas A&M University-College Station*
Texas A&M University-Corpus Christi
Texas A&M University-Kingsville

Texas Christian University
Texas Southern University
Texas State University
Texas Tech University
Thomas Jefferson University
Tufts University
Tulane University of Louisiana
University at Albany, SUNY*
University at Buffalo, SUNY
The University of Akron Main Campus
The University of Alabama
The University of Alabama at Birmingham
The University of Alabama in Huntsville
University of Alaska Fairbanks
The University of Arizona*
University of Arkansas
University of Arkansas at Little Rock
University of California, Berkeley*
University of California, Davis*
University of California, Irvine*
University of California, Los Angeles*
University of California, Merced*
University of California, Riverside*
University of California, San Diego*
University of California, Santa Barbara*
University of California, Santa Cruz*
University of Central Florida*
The University of Chicago
University of Cincinnati
University of Colorado Boulder*
University of Colorado Colorado Springs
University of Colorado Denver/Anschutz
  Medical Campus
University of Connecticut
University of Dayton
University of Delaware*
University of Denver
University of Florida*
University of Georgia*
University of Hawai'i at Mānoa
University of Houston
University of Idaho
University of Illinois Chicago*

University of Illinois Urbana-Champaign*
The University of Iowa*
The University of Kansas*
University of Kentucky*
University of Louisiana at Lafayette
University of Louisville
University of Maine
University of Maryland Eastern Shore
University of Maryland, Baltimore County
University of Maryland, College Park*
University of Massachusetts Amherst
University of Massachusetts Boston
University of Massachusetts Dartmouth
University of Massachusetts Lowell
The University of Memphis*
University of Miami*
University of Michigan–Ann Arbor*
University of Minnesota Twin Cities*
The University of Mississippi*
University of Missouri-Columbia*
University of Missouri–Kansas City
University of Missouri–St. Louis
University of Montana
University of Nebraska at Omaha
University of Nebraska–Lincoln*
University of Nevada, Las Vegas
University of Nevada, Reno*
University of New England
University of New Hampshire*
The University of New Mexico*
University of New Orleans
The University of North Carolina at
  Chapel Hill*
The University of North Carolina Charlotte*
The University of North Carolina Greensboro
The University of North Carolina Wilmington
University of North Dakota
University of North Florida
University of North Texas
University of Notre Dame*
The University of Oklahoma-Norman Campus
University of Oregon*
University of Pennsylvania

University of Pittsburgh-Pittsburgh Campus*
University of Puerto Rico-Rio Piedras Campus
University of Rhode Island
University of Rochester*
University of San Diego
University of South Alabama
University of South Carolina Columbia*
University of South Dakota
University of South Florida*
University of Southern California
The University of Southern Mississippi
The University of Tennessee Knoxville*
The University of Texas at Arlington*
The University of Texas at Austin*
The University of Texas at Dallas*
The University of Texas at El Paso*
The University of Texas at San Antonio*
The University of Texas at Tyler*
The University of Texas Rio Grande Valley*
The University of Toledo*
The University of Tulsa
The University of Utah*
University of Vermont

University of Virginia*
University of Washington-Seattle Campus*
University of Wisconsin-Madison
University of Wisconsin-Milwaukee
University of Wyoming*
Utah State University*
Vanderbilt University*
Villanova University
Virginia Commonwealth University*
Virginia Polytechnic Institute and State
    University*
Wake Forest University
Washington State University*
Washington University in St. Louis*
Wayne State University
West Chester University of Pennsylvania
West Virginia University*
Western Michigan University
Wichita State University
William & Mary
Worcester Polytechnic Institute
Wright State University
Yale University

Appendix D. Boyer 2030 Commission Information Sessions with National Experts

The Boyer 2030 Commission and its sponsor, The Association for Undergraduate Education at Research Universities (UERU), gratefully acknowledges the vital input of nationally leading experts who in 2021 and 2022 generously shared their perspectives with the Commission and with Undergraduate Vice Provosts/Presidents (UVPs), who are UERU's principal constituents.

MIT's First-Year Grading Policy

Ian Waitz, Vice Chancellor for Undergraduate and Graduate Education, Massachusetts Institute of Technology

Kate Weishaar, First-Year Experience Project Coordinator, Massachusetts Institute of Technology

Educating for World Readiness

David Carballo, Assistant Provost for General Education, Boston University

Cathy Davidson, Founding Director, The Futures Initiative, CUNY

Abraham Goldberg, Inaugural Director, James Madison Center for Civic Engagement, James Madison University

Melinda Zook, Director, Cornerstone Integrated Liberal Arts, Purdue University

Analytics & Assessment for Equity & Excellence

Greg Heileman, Vice Provost for Undergraduate Education, University of Arizona

Jillian Kinzie, Associate Director, Center for Postsecondary Research & National Survey of Student Engagement (NSSE) Institute, School of Education, Indiana University-Bloomington

Tim Renick, Executive Director, National Institute for Student Success (NISS), Georgia State University

Leading the Way for Equity & Excellence—UTEP & Morgan State

Heather Wilson, President, The University of Texas at El Paso

John Wiebe, Provost & Vice President for Academic Affairs, University of Texas at El Paso

Tiffany Mfume, Assistant Vice President for Student Success and Retention, Morgan State University

Leading the Way for Equity & Excellence—Meyerhoff Scholars

Keith Harmon, Director, Meyerhoff Scholars Program, University of Maryland, Baltimore County

Digital Transformation for Equity & Excellence

Lisa McIntyre, Assistant Vice Provost for Student Success Innovations, Arizona State University

Bobby Gray, Director of Digital Transformation, Arizona State University

Tim McKay, Associate Dean of Undergraduate Education, Director of SEISMIC, University of Michigan

Marco Molinaro, Assistant Vice Provost for Educational Effectiveness, University of California, Davis

Bror Saxberg, former Vice President for Learning Science, Chan Zuckerberg Initiative

Holistic Advising for Equity & Excellence

Richard Light, Carl H. Pforzheimer Jr. Professor of Teaching & Learning at Harvard Graduate School of Education, Harvard University

Campus Freedom of Speech & Expression

Tony Frank, Chancellor, Colorado State University System

Reform of Faculty Roles & Incentive Structures

Adrianna Kezar, Wilbur Kieffer Endowed Professor, Dean's Professor of Leadership, Director of the Pullias Center, Director of the Delphi Project, University of Southern California

Mental Health & Well-Being

Bernadette Melnyk, Vice President for Health Promotion, Chief Wellness Officer, The Ohio State University

José Villalba, Vice President for Diversity & Inclusion, Chief Diversity Officer, Wake Forest University

ACE's Reimagining Transfer for Student Success

Louis Soares, Chief Learning & Innovation Officer, American Council on Education

HBCU Research University Leaders on the Equity/Excellence Imperative

Melanie Carter, Associate Provost & Director of the Center for HBCU Research, Leadership, and Policy, Howard University

Kenneth Anderson, Associate Provost for Undergraduate Studies, Howard University

John P. Gardner, Assistant Vice President for Academic Engagement and Student Success, Prairie View A&M

Kara Turner, Vice President for Enrollment Management and Student Success, Morgan State University

Tiffany Mfume, Associate Vice President, Student Success and Retention, Morgan State University

Alicia Simon, General Education Curriculum Faculty Coordinator, Clark Atlanta University